# FIRE ON ICE

## The New Jersey Devils' Road to the 2003 Stanley Cup Championship

SPORTS PUBLISHING L.L.C.

www.sportspublishingllc.com

# FIRE ON ICE
## The New Jersey Devils' Road to the 2003 Stanley Cup Championship

PETER L. BANNON, Publisher

JOSEPH J. BANNON, JR. AND SUSAN M. MOYER, Senior managing editors

GABE A. ROSEN AND KIPP A. WILFONG, Developmental editors

JENNIFER L. POLSON, Book design

JENNIFER L. POLSON AND TRACY GAUDREAU, Book layout

CHRISTINE F. MOHRBACHER, Cover design

TRACY GAUDREAU, Photo imaging

CYNTHIA L. McNEW, Copy editor

ISBN: 1-58261-641-8

SPORTS PUBLISHING L.L.C.
www.sportspublishingllc.com

# CONTENTS

NEW JERSEY PRIDE ................................ 8
PROFILE: PAT BURNS .......................... 14

**REGULAR SEASON**
GAME OF THE MONTH: OCTOBER ........ 16
  OCTOBER 10, 2002
PROFILE: MARTIN BRODEUR .............. 22
GAME OF THE MONTH: NOVEMBER ...... 24
  NOVEMBER 7, 2002
PROFILE: SCOTT STEVENS .................. 30
GAME OF THE MONTH: DECEMBER ...... 32
  DECEMBER 19, 2002
PROFILE: KEN DANEYKO .................... 38
GAME OF THE MONTH: JANUARY .......... 40
  JANUARY 18, 2003
PROFILE: JAY PANDOLFO .................... 46
GAME OF THE MONTH: FEBRUARY ........ 48
  FEBRUARY 12, 2003
PROFILE: SERGIE BRYLIN .................... 54
GAME OF THE MONTH: MARCH ............ 56
  MARCH 30, 2003
PROFILE: SCOTT GOMEZ .................... 62
GAME OF THE MONTH: APRIL .............. 64
  APRIL 4, 2003

**PLAYOFFS**
**ROUND 1** ........................................ 70
GAME 1 .......................................... 72
  APRIL 9, 2003
GAME 2 .......................................... 76
  APRIL 11, 2003
GAME 3 .......................................... 80
  APRIL 13, 2003
GAME 4 .......................................... 82
  APRIL 15, 2003
GAME 5 .......................................... 84
  APRIL 17, 2003

**ROUND 2** ........................................ 88
GAME 1 .......................................... 90
  APRIL 24, 2003

GAME 2 .......................................... 94
  APRIL 26, 2003
GAME 3 .......................................... 96
  APRIL 28, 2003
GAME 4 .......................................... 98
  APRIL 30, 2003
GAME 5 ........................................ 100
  MAY 2, 2003

**ROUND 3** ...................................... 104
GAME 1 ........................................ 106
  MAY 10, 2003
GAME 2 ........................................ 108
  MAY 13, 2003
GAME 3 ........................................ 112
  MAY 15, 2003
GAME 4 ........................................ 116
  MAY 17, 2003
GAME 5 ........................................ 120
  MAY 19, 2003
GAME 6 ........................................ 122
  MAY 21, 2003
GAME 7 ........................................ 124
  MAY 23, 2003

**STANLEY CUP FINALS** .................. 128
GAME 1 ........................................ 130
  MAY 27, 2003
GAME 2 ........................................ 134
  MAY 29, 2003
GAME 3 ........................................ 138
  MAY 31, 2003
GAME 4 ........................................ 142
  JUNE 2, 2003
GAME 5 ........................................ 146
  JUNE 5, 2003
GAME 6 ........................................ 150
  JUNE 7, 2003
GAME 7 ........................................ 154
  JUNE 9, 2003

**REGULAR SEASON STATISTICS** ...... 160

# Nets, Devils Share Arena and Jersey Pride, Not Much Else

**JOSEPH WHITE, AP SPORTS WRITER**

EAST RUTHERFORD, N.J.—Yes, the New Jersey Nets are aware that their arena-mates, the New Jersey Devils, are in the Stanley Cup finals.

But that's about all they know about the hockey team.

"Don't ask me to name three Devils," Nets coach Byron Scott said with a chuckle. "Stevenson, toughest guy on the team, I know that. I can't pronounce it, but the goalie, I love the way he plays. He got them in the finals; that's all that matters."

As vague as that sounds, Scott was better informed than most of his players Saturday morning as the Nets prepared to emulate their Meadowlands brethren. New Jersey—basketball version—looked to finish a sweep of the Detroit Pistons on Saturday night to advance to the NBA Finals, one day after New Jersey—hockey version—did the NHL equivalent with a victory over the Ottawa Senators.

"It shows we've got some pretty good teams here in Jersey," Scott said. "The organization can be very proud of that."

Scott and players Richard Jefferson, Kenyon Martin and Lucious Harris all said they had never seen a hockey game live. Jefferson at least had one advantage over his coach: He could pronounce the goalie's name.

"When we're playing, they're on the road," Jefferson said. "But I have seen the inside of their locker room. I'm trying to steal a Martin Brodeur jersey, but the equipment guy won't let me.

"I don't know much about hockey, but I know they're good. I know they're the one thing Jersey had to hang their hat on before Jason Kidd and the rest of us got here, so it's good to join the party."

For Martin, the whole Nets-Devils, Jersey-pride, finals-together thing was a bit of a stretch.

"It'd be cool, I guess," Martin said. "They already won them a title, so we have to win ours."

Harris was happy just to correctly guess the number of periods in a hockey game.

"Three periods? That's right?" Harris said. "I don't skate."

"It shows we've got some **pretty good teams** here in Jersey. The organization can be **very proud of that.**"

—NEW JERSEY NETS COACH BYRON SCOTT

AP/WWP

AP/WWP

Scott was asked whether a dual national spotlight might help educate the rest of the country about the swampy northern end of the Garden State.

"I've learned everything I need to know about Jersey," said Scott, a California native in his third season with the team. "All I need to know is coming down 280 to the Jersey 'Pike to the office and the arena is always a pretty good trip. And I love *The Sopranos*."

With the Nets facing the possibility of a long break before the start of the NBA Finals, Scott might finally have a chance to see the Devils in person when they host Games 1 and 2 of the Stanley Cup finals Tuesday and Thursday.

"I'll have to go," Scott said. "I've heard it's much better in person anyway."

Jefferson, though, suddenly curbed his Devils enthusiasm when it was suggested he could go, taking a quite a pause before giving his answer.

"Yeah, I wouldn't mind going," Jefferson said. "I wouldn't be able to watch too much of the game if I sat in the middle of the stands, so I might just have to check them out on TV."

# PAT BURNS

POSITION **HEAD COACH** • NAMED COACH **JUNE 13, 2002** • BORN **ST. HENRI, QUEBEC**

## DEVILS FIRE CONSTANTINE, HIRE BURNS AS COACH

TOM CANAVAN, AP SPORTS WRITER

EAST RUTHERFORD, N.J.—Hanging around with George Steinbrenner is starting to rub off on Lou Lamoriello.

The boss of the New Jersey Devils is now just as quick on the draw as Steinbrenner when it comes to dumping coaches who don't succeed.

Kevin Constantine became Lamoriello's latest victim on Thursday, when he was fired and replaced by Pat Burns, just over a month after the team was eliminated in the first round of the NHL playoffs.

"The personality of our organization is not to wait," said Lamoriello, who hired Constantine to replace Larry Robinson in January. "We have raised the bar. We expect to win, and that's on everyone."

The coaching switch is the fourth in four years for the Devils, who won the Stanley Cup in 2000 and came within a game of repeating the following season.

Lamoriello said the six-game loss to Carolina in the first round of the playoffs this year was just one factor in his decision to make the change. He indicated that Constantine did not get enough out of the talent on the Devils' roster.

It's the same type of justification Steinbrenner used with the New York Yankees when he had a managerial merry-go-round in the 1970s and '80s.

As the chief executive for YankeeNets, the corporation that runs the Devils and New Jersey Nets of the NBA, Lamoriello and Steinbrenner work together.

Lamoriello decided to make the change over the last two weeks. He said he did not meet with his players before making his decision.

"Looking over the picture of where we have raised the bar here in our organization and what we are expecting out of our players, I felt a certain individual and a certain type of coach was needed, and I felt Pat Burns fit that description right to the T," Lamoriello said.

Constantine said in a teleconference Thursday that he learned of Lamoriello's decision earlier this week.

"It's disappointing," Constantine said. "We had a good run during the regular season, and obviously we were disappointed during the playoffs. Beyond that, we were looking forward to having a full season, a full training camp."

Constantine said he planned to meet with Lamoriello in the next week to discuss his future with the organization.

A three-time NHL Coach of the Year, Burns has not been behind the bench since being fired by the Boston Bruins eight games into the 2000-01 season.

He takes over a club that finished sixth in the Eastern Conference at 41-28-9-4. The Devils' 95 points were 16 fewer than the previous season, when they were the conference's best team.

"I don't think there is a whole lot to clean up here," said Burns, who has the reputation as a disciplinarian.

"I think I am fair," Burns said. "To say I am a strict disciplinarian, I think fair is the right word. Everyone has rules to follow and you expect everyone to follow them."

Lamoriello has shown little patience with his coaches in recent years.

Robbie Ftorek replaced Jacques Lemaire for the 1998-99 season. Robinson replaced Ftorek late in the 1999-2000 season and led the Devils to their second Stanley Cup since 1995.

With the Devils in danger of missing the 2001-2002 playoffs, Constantine replaced Robinson. New Jersey was 20-9-2 under Constantine in the regular season before being eliminated in the playoffs by the Hurricanes.

Burns has worked as a radio analyst in Montreal and Toronto and for a Los Angeles Kings minor-league team since being fired by Boston. He has a 412-314-129 record in 11-plus coaching seasons, winning NHL Coach of the Year awards in 1989 with Montreal, 1993 with Toronto and 1998 with Boston.

"I don't know what to say," Devils forward Scott Gomez said. "It's obviously too bad for Kevin. But you look at Pat Burns's record and it speaks for itself."

Devils goaltender Martin Brodeur was surprised and excited.

"I think this will help us," he said. "He knows the game, and he's not going to let stuff slip, on the ice or off the ice. He's got that aura. He commands respect."

AP/WWP

# Madden, Brodeur Shut Down Senators

**IRA PODELL, AP SPORTS WRITER**

OTTAWA—John Madden's first goal of the season nearly went unnoticed, so he made sure he buried his second one.

Madden scored twice, and Martin Brodeur came within 1:14 of a shutout as the New Jersey Devils beat the Ottawa Senators 2-1 on Thursday night in the NHL opener for both teams.

A video review was needed to confirm Madden's first goal early in the second period. Play continued for another 28 seconds before the play was reviewed after his shot 2:28 into the period beat goalie Patrick Lalime and went right through the net's mesh.

"When it's your first of the year, you're like, 'It's in!'" Madden said. "I let it go, I just watched it, and I saw it go underneath the crossbar and I was like, 'What the heck happened there?' I'm not sure if it was faulty netting or a hard shot."

There was no mistaking his second of the game, a short-handed effort with 1:21 left in the period.

"I put that one in the middle of the net," Madden said of his breakaway shot through Lalime's legs, which put the Devils up 2-0.

| FINAL | 1st | 2nd | 3rd | T |
|---|---|---|---|---|
| New Jersey | 0 | 2 | 0 | 2 |
| Ottawa | 0 | 0 | 1 | 1 |

Brodeur made 33 saves, losing his shutout on Ottawa's 32nd shot when Daniel Alfredsson tipped in Petr Schastlivy's shot 18:46 into the third.

Schastlivy had another chance moments later, but Brodeur stopped him as New Jersey held on to win in head coach Pat Burns's debut with the Devils.

"The first one's always a tough one," said Burns, who last coached with Boston in 2000-01.

Senators center Mike Fisher also got a shot past Brodeur early in the second, but his drive rang off the right post.

"We created chances but couldn't bury them when we needed to," Fisher said. "Their goaltender was the story tonight, I guess."

The Devils came back down the ice, and Madden beat Lalime with the shot that went right through the mesh at the bottom of the net just inside the right post.

As play continued, Madden gestured toward the net, indicating that the puck had gone through the net, and the replay officials agreed, stunning the Corel Centre crowd of 16,865 as the clock was reset from 17:04 to 17:32.

"We had a great angle from the bench," Devils left wing Patrik Elias said. "It wouldn't have been possible for the net to move like that if it didn't go through. It's pretty strange because it was a brand new net."

Madden made it 2-0 with an unassisted goal during a Senators power play 18:46 into the second. Madden intercepted Ottawa defenseman Wade Redden's backhand pass at the Senators' blue line and drove in on a breakaway, beating Lalime through the pads for an unassisted goal.

AP/WWP

## October Results

| Thu. Oct. 10 | at Senators | W 2-1 | 1-0-0-0 |
|---|---|---|---|
| Sat. Oct. 12 | Blue Jackets | W 3-2 | 2-0-0-0 |
| Fri. Oct. 18 | Predators | W 3-2 | 3-0-0-0 |
| Sat. Oct. 19 | at Hurricanes | L 1-3 | 3-1-0-0 |
| Wed. Oct. 23 | at Thrashers | W 2-1 | 4-1-0-0 |
| Fri. Oct. 25 | at Sabres | W 2-1 | 5-1-0-0 |
| Sat. Oct. 26 | Lightning | W 5-1 | 6-1-0-0 |
| Tue. Oct. 29 | Hurricanes | L 1-2 | 6-2-0-0 |

# MARTIN BRODEUR

NO. 30 • HEIGHT 6'2 • WEIGHT 210 • POSITION G • CATCHES LEFT • BORN MAY 6, 1972 • BORN MONTREAL, QUEBEC

## MARTIN BRODEUR TALKS ABOUT HIS ONETIME IDOL—PATRICK ROY

TOM CANAVAN, AP SPORTS WRITER

WEST ORANGE, N.J.—Being the son of the team photographer for the Montreal Canadiens had its advantages for Martin Brodeur.

The wall of his room never lacked for photographs of his favorite goaltenders.

Always big goaltenders, though, just like the young Canadian teenager who was hanging up the pictures.

No one in the gallery stood out more than Brodeur's idol, Patrick Roy. He was special. Not only was he good, he was the hero of Montreal.

Brodeur still recalls their first meeting.

"I was at The Forum and my father had to do a photo shoot," Brodeur said. "I got a chance to meet him briefly while I was helping out my dad. My father had been bringing me around a lot, so it wasn't like I went crazy. It was kind of nice to see him. When you see someone as an athlete and you see him play hockey, it's a lot different when you see him in person."

In the years since that meeting, Roy left the Canadiens under difficult circumstances, joined

the Colorado Avalanche and led them to a Stanley Cup in 1996.

Brodeur has written his own page in sports history. Since joining the Devils full-time in 1993-94, he has led them to Stanley Cups in 1995 and 2000, and he is on the verge of doing it again.

But in 2001, Roy and the Avalanche stood in the way.

"Definitely it's an exciting time," Brodeur said in May of that same year. "Not just playing in the Stanley Cup, but playing against him. He has the reputation of being one of the clutch goalies, and we'll have a chance to face him and beat him. It's a great opportunity for everybody."

Roy might have been the biggest reason the Avalanche were back in the Cup finals for the first time since 1996, when they swept Florida. Prior to the finals, Roy posted a 12-4 record with a1.74 goals against average and a .932 save percentage in the playoffs.

Brodeur posted a 12-6 record and allowed 33 goals in a postseason where he tied a league record with four shutouts. He was also heavily criticized every time he seemingly let in a goal, but Brodeur always knew that came with the territory of playing goal for a great defensive team.

But Brodeur didn't have many sleepless nights fretting a head-to-head showdown with his boyhood idol.

"It's the last thing I think of," Brodeur said after a 30-minute practice at the Devils' South Mountain facility. "You don't want to get into challenges. I think, personally, you don't want to put too much pressure into the situation.

"For me, I'm playing for the Devils and I can't go out and score on him," Brodeur added. "I have enough to worry about, with all these great players on the other side, than to worry about the guy who is trying to stop our players."

Roy, who was driven from the nets twice in the Devils' two regular-season wins over Colorado in 2001, didn't speak much with the media.

AP/WWP

That didn't surprise Brodeur. He had gotten to know the goaltender playing at All-Star games and being teammates on the Canadian Olympic team. The two weren't close friends, but they talked occasionally.

Brodeur is no longer the wide-eyed 16-year-old who first met Roy while helping out his father at a photography session.

Brodeur is one of the best goaltenders in the NHL, just like Roy.

"Now I'm playing against a great goalie and it's a fun thing," Brodeur said before the series. "It's a fun

thing for me. It's a big challenge any time I meet a great goaltender. These are things that stay with you, and you want to play well against the big goalie because you know they won't give you anything."

Former Devils coach Larry Robinson told Brodeur to forget the two regular-season games in which New Jersey outscored Colorado 12-4.

"You can get by with certain things in the year, but when playoffs roll around he [Roy] is a different goaltender," Robinson said. "He loves the challenge. He is like our guy. The tougher the challenge, the better they play."

# Brodeur Shuts Down Flyers

**ROB MAADDI, AP SPORTS WRITER**

PHILADELPHIA—Martin Brodeur doesn't need a lot of offensive support.

Brodeur stopped 23 shots, and Jamie Langenbrunner scored with 7:43 left as the New Jersey Devils snapped the Philadelphia Flyers' six-game winning streak with a 1-0 victory on Thursday night in the first meeting of the season between the Atlantic Division rivals.

It was Brodeur's 56th career shutout, first this season and ninth by a 1-0 margin. He has allowed just 17 goals in 11 games, fewest in the NHL.

"It was a game to see how we would match up against the league's best team, and we did real well," Brodeur said. "Defensively we were awesome, and offensively we didn't have much, but it was enough."

The Flyers are off to a 9-2-2 start under new coach Ken Hitchcock. New Jersey is 8-3 under its new coach Pat Burns.

After Philadelphia defenseman Eric Desjardins failed to control the puck near the right boards,

| FINAL | 1st | 2nd | 3rd | T |
|---|---|---|---|---|
| New Jersey | 0 | 0 | 1 | 1 |
| Philadelphia | 0 | 0 | 0 | 0 |

Langenbrunner gathered it, skated just outside the right circle and fired a shot into the top left corner for his third goal.

"I tried to move the puck and it got stuck on the boards and I missed," Desjardins said. "He came off the bench and he was flying. He went right for the puck and made a perfect shot."

Seconds earlier, Brodeur stopped Simon Gagne on a two-on-one breakaway.

"I didn't want to move," Brodeur said of his strategy. "I played with the guy in the Olympics. He likes to make the goalie make the first move. I stood my ground."

The Devils didn't allow the Flyers to get a shot during five power-play opportunities, including a five-on-three.

"Brodeur is probably our best defensemen right now," Burns said.

Desjardins nearly beat Brodeur with a slap shot early in the game. The puck got past Brodeur, but he reached back and stopped it as it was heading into the net.

The Flyers had a two-man advantage for 1:19 early in the second period, but failed to even get a shot on Brodeur. Philadelphia is two for 31 on the power play in its last five games.

"We were just trying not to let them set up for a one-timer because they have some guys who can shoot it off the pass," Devils center Joe Nieuwendyk said. "Down two men, it looked dismal in a game like this that late."

Flyers goalie Roman Cechmanek stopped 26 shots, including a sprawling save on a shot by Jeff Friesen midway through the second period.

"You don't want to lose a game because of a bouncing puck, but we've won some games that way," Hitchcock said. "It was ours for the taking in the third period."

AP/WWP

# November Results

| Sat. Nov. 2 | Blackhawks | W 5-1 | 7-2-0-0 |
| Tue. Nov. 5 | Flames | L 2-3 | 7-3-0-0 |
| Thu. Nov. 7 | at Flyers | W 1-0 | 8-3-0-0 |
| Sat. Nov. 9 | Oilers | L 3-6 | 8-4-0-0 |
| Tue. Nov. 12 | Mighty Ducks | W 3-2 | 9-4-0-0 |
| Fri. Nov. 15 | Canadiens | W 5-1 | 10-4-0-0 |
| Sat. Nov. 16 | at Canadiens | L 1-3 | 10-5-0-0 |
| Tue. Nov. 19 | Sabres | W 4-3 | 11-5-0-0 |
| Thu. Nov. 21 | Rangers | T 4-4 | 11-5-1-0 |
| Sat. Nov. 23 | Lightning | L 1-3 | 11-6-1-0 |
| Wed. Nov. 27 | at Red Wings | OTL 2-3 | 11-6-1-1 |
| Fri. Nov. 29 | at Predators | W 2-1 | 12-6-1-1 |
| Sat. Nov. 30 | at Blues | W 5-4 | 13-6-1-1 |

# SCOTT STEVENS

NO. **4** • HEIGHT **6'2** • WEIGHT **215** • POSITION **D** • SHOOTS **LEFT** • BORN **APRIL 1, 1964** • BORN **KITCHENER, ONTARIO**

## STEVENS GETTING BETTER WITH AGE

TOM CANAVAN, AP SPORTS WRITER

WEST ORANGE, N.J.—In the opening minutes of practice Thursday, Scott Stevens stood opposite Jamie Langenbrunner, waiting to pounce on a rebound.

As the puck hit off goaltender Corey Schwab's pads, the Devils teammates acted like kids on the first day of training camp, straining to be the first to slam the puck in the net.

It was hard to tell who got it, but Stevens smiled broadly as he skated hard to get back to center ice.

Stevens is not only enjoying his 21st season in the NHL, the 39-year-old defenseman is still the force driving the Devils to another Stanley Cup run. They start the best-of-seven Eastern Conference finals Saturday in Ottawa.

"Every year he comes in and he's in the best shape of anyone in the locker room," Devils goaltender Martin Brodeur said. "He is our leader, but it's more than just a leader. He's an example of what a professional athlete should be. The way he prepares and goes out and battles at this stage in his career. That's what guys are most impressed with."

Stevens has been phenomenal in the first two rounds of the playoffs. He leads the league with a plus-10 ranking despite missing most of Game 3 of the conference semifinals after being hit in the ear with a shot.

It's a remarkable statistic because the offensively challenged Devils have only played 10 postseason games, and Stevens always goes against an opponent's top line.

He seemingly was on the ice every time Joe Thornton was in for the Boston Bruins in the first round and he was out there when Vincent Lecavalier hit the ice for Tampa Bay in the conference semifinals.

It remains to be seen whom Stevens will face against the Senators. Ottawa has scorers on almost every line. The most likely choice would be against the line that has Marian Hossa, who leads Ottawa with five goals and seven assists.

Hossa, who has struggled in recent playoffs, has surpassed his previous best of four goals in a 12-game run last year.

'Last year was probably the first playoff where [Hossa] competed well and took it to another level. This year, he kept progressing," Senators coach Jacques Martin said.

Center John Madden knows Stevens will be ready.

"The one thing I have always admired about Scotty is the way he prepares for a hockey game," Madden said. "He has accomplished a lot in his career, yet he comes to the rink and still works on the fundamentals of hockey."

Hot-tempered as a youngster, Stevens has matured after two decades in the league.

"Sometimes the older a player gets, the smarter he gets," coach Pat Burns said. "You learn how to use your ice. You learn how to use your time and how to use your space."

Stevens just smiles when asked about his age. His face may be weathered and there are scars, but he doesn't play like an old man. He continues to be among the Devils' leaders in minutes played.

"Age is just a number," said Stevens, who led the Devils to Stanley Cups in 1995 and 2000. "It's how you feel, what you do to take care of yourself and how you like the game. I enjoy the game. I enjoy the competition. I enjoy challenging age, if that's going to be a factor. I'm looking forward to it."

Brodeur cited one more key to Stevens's success: his ability to play under control.

AP/WWP

"He plays within his own skills and doesn't try to do too much out there," Brodeur said. "If a lot of players tried to follow what he does, they'd be a lot more successful."

# Devils, Nieuwendyk Halt Streaks

ALAN ROBINSON, AP SPORTS WRITER

**P**ITTSBURGH—Joe Nieuwendyk finally stopped a seemingly endless streak and kept the Pittsburgh Penguins on one that soon might reach historical proportions.

Nieuwendyk scored his first goal in 21 games and set up New Jersey's second goal with an uncontested faceoff win, and the Devils ran Pittsburgh's losing streak to a near-record 10 games by winning 3-1 Thursday night.

Oleg Tverdovsky and Brian Gionta also scored as New Jersey, a lethargic 3-0 loser to Ottawa at home Wednesday, stopped a three-game losing streak—and, at least for one night, rumors Nieuwendyk might be traded.

Nieuwendyk, a former Stanley Cup star for Dallas, scored a day after Devils general manager Lou Lamoriello expressed confidence that he was about to come out of his slump. Nieuwendyk hadn't scored since Nov. 2 against Chicago.

"I don't know if I didn't let it get to me, but I've always been a firm believer in good things will happen eventually," Nieuwendyk said. "I struggled

| FINAL | 1st | 2nd | 3rd | T |
|---|---|---|---|---|
| New Jersey | 1 | 2 | 0 | 3 |
| Pittsburgh | 1 | 0 | 0 | 1 |

with my confidence, but hopefully, this will jump-start some things."

With Nieuwendyk finally contributing, the Devils ran the Penguins' losing streak to within one of the franchise record.

According to the Elias Sports Bureau, the Penguins have had only one longer losing streak in their 35-year history, an 11-game streak from Jan. 22, 1983, through Feb. 10, 1983, the year before Mario Lemieux arrived.

"I've been through some tough times here," Lemieux said. "We just need to win a game to regain our confidence and get some key guys back so we get back to where it was earlier in the season, when we were playing well and there was a lot of excitement."

What makes the current streak significant is Lemieux is healthy and playing, although he went a

third straight game without scoring. Until Tuesday, when he didn't score in a 5-2 loss at Phoenix, the NHL's leading scorer hadn't gone more than one game without a point.

"It's difficult when you're making a lot of changes like we've been making," Lemieux said. "We're playing a lot of new guys and we keep making the same mistakes every night."

The Penguins haven't won since beating Buffalo 4-1 Nov. 29, losing their last six on the road and their last four at home. Their lineup has been depleted by injuries that have cost them two of their top four scorers, forward Aleksey Morozov and defenseman Dick Tarnstrom, and at one point sidelined more than 40 percent of their veteran players.

Since starting 7-2-2, the Penguins are only 4-12-1-4.

The Penguins took a 1-0 lead with 3:08 gone, a rarity during the streak, on Milan Kraft's first goal of the season. But, obviously weary from a winless five-game road trip, they managed only 15 more shots on Devils goaltender Martin Brodeur.

Nieuwendyk tied it about 10 minutes later, stealing an ill-advised pass from along the left-wing boards by Ville Nieminen and quickly stuffing a shot past Jean-Sebastien Aubin.

Nieuwendyk then set up Tverdovsky's third of the season, a slap shot from the right point past a screened Aubin early in the second. Nieuwendyk won the faceoff uncontested when the puck was dropped before the Penguins' Randy Robitaille arrived in the circle.

"I skated from the bench right there," Robitaille said. "He's got to realize that. It boggles my mind he would do that. I know they're trying to speed up the game, but this isn't the preseason. This was a big game for us and that obviously was a huge goal."

Gionta got his seventh midway through the period, a seemingly harmless shot from along the goal line that deflected off defenseman Jamie Pushor's skate and into the net.

# December Results

| | | | |
|---|---|---|---|
| Mon. Dec. 2 | at Flyers | W 1-0 | 14-6-1-1 |
| Wed. Dec. 4 | Canucks | OTL 2-3 | 14-6-1-2 |
| Fri. Dec. 6 | Penguins | W 3-1 | 15-6-1-2 |
| Sat. Dec. 7 | at Maple Leafs | L 0-1 | 15-7-1-2 |
| Tue. Dec. 10 | Blues | W 2-0 | 16-7-1-2 |
| Thu. Dec. 12 | at Blue Jackets | L 2-4 | 16-8-1-2 |
| Sat. Dec. 14 | at Senators | OTL 3-4 | 16-8-1-3 |
| Wed. Dec. 18 | Senators | L 0-3 | 16-9-1-3 |
| Thu. Dec. 19 | at Penguins | W 3-1 | 17-9-1-3 |
| Sat. Dec. 21 | Stars | W 5-3 | 18-9-1-3 |
| Mon. Dec. 23 | at Rangers | T 2-2 | 18-9-2-3 |
| Fri. Dec. 27 | at Capitals | L 2-3 | 18-10-2-3 |
| Sat. Dec. 28 | Capitals | W 2-1 | 19-10-2-3 |
| Mon. Dec. 30 | at Bruins | W 1-0 | 20-10-2-3 |

" I don't know if I didn't let it get to me, but I've always been a firm believer in good things will happen eventually. I struggled with my confidence, but hopefully, this will jump-start some things."

—DEVILS CENTER JOE NIEUWENDYK

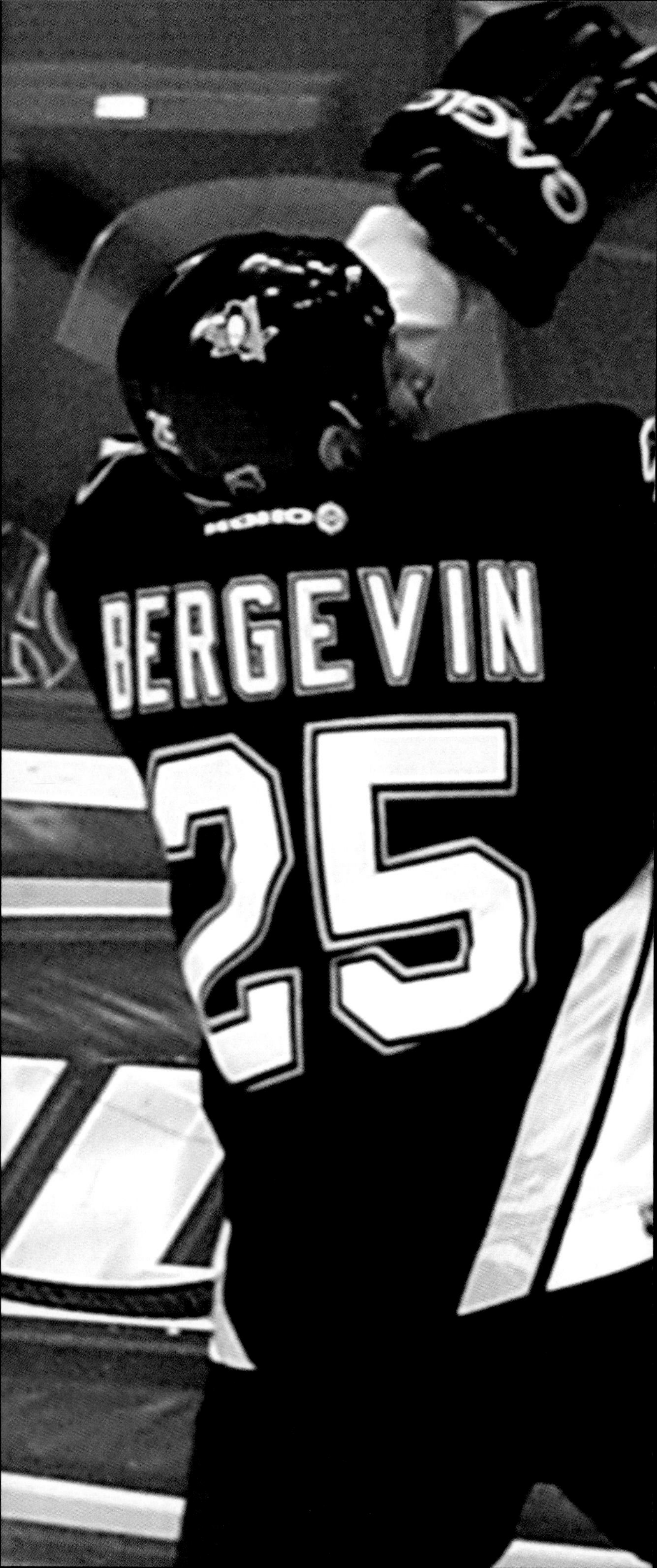

AP/WWP

# KEN DANEYKO

NO. 3 • HEIGHT **6'1** • WEIGHT **215** • POSITION **D** • SHOOTS **LEFT** • BORN **APRIL 17, 1964** • BORN **WINDSOR, ONTARIO**

## DANEYKO HOPING TO GET BACK INTO DEVILS LINEUP

TOM CANAVAN, AP SPORTS WRITER

EAST RUTHERFORD, N.J.—Ken Daneyko's downcast feelings come through clearly in his voice.

While thrilled the New Jersey Devils are one win away from their fourth Stanley Cup finals, Daneyko is going through one of the most difficult periods in his 18 NHL seasons.

For the first time in his career, Daneyko is sitting during the playoffs. The rugged defenseman has been a healthy scratch the past four games of the Eastern Conference finals and has no idea whether he will play Wednesday when New Jersey can eliminate the Ottawa Senators at home.

"Sure, it's disappointing," Daneyko said Tuesday. "No matter who you are, if it's not disappointing you shouldn't be in this league. Having said that, I understood coming in that this might be a possibility. It doesn't make it any easier. We have a great opportunity and I am just staying positive."

After taking off his equipment after practice, Daneyko sat in front of his locker and waited.

One by one, reporters stopped by and asked Daneyko if he knew when he'd be back in the lineup in the wake of New Jersey's 3-1 loss in Game 5, a setback that cut the Devils' lead to 3-2 in the best-of-seven series.

"I have no idea," Daneyko said.

"Sorry, I can't help you," he said the next time.

Until this year, Daneyko had played in every postseason game for New Jersey, helping the club win two Stanley Cups and reach Game 7 in the 2001 finals.

The streak ended at 165 games when coach Pat Burns sat Daneyko for Game 4 against Boston in the first round. New Jersey was crushed that night.

Daneyko played the final game against the Bruins, each of the five games against Tampa Bay in the second round, and the opener against Ottawa—an overtime loss. He and Oleg Tverdovsky were on the ice for a couple of goals in that game, and Burns replaced them in Game 2 with Richard Smehlik and Tommy Albelin.

New Jersey won the next three games before losing Monday.

On game night, Daneyko has tried to stay out of the picture. He sits in the locker room and watches the action on television. If he sees something, the 39-year-old player doesn't hesitate to offer advice.

"He's been very positive," captain Scott Stevens said. "He's handled it very well. It makes it easy for everyone in this room to talk about it. Everyone is behind Kenny. He is a competitor and a leader on this team. I'm sure he'll get a chance to get back on."

Burns would not discuss his lineup on Tuesday.

"I am not going to specu-late," Daneyko said. "It's too hard to guess. You guess and that can really mess with your mind. I'm just waiting and staying posi-tive. I'll be ready if called upon."

AP/WWP

While the Devils will have two chances to elimi-nate the Senators, they don't want to go back to Ottawa for a deciding game.

"It's something we have to put in our minds, that we need to do this now," goaltender Martin Brodeur said. "From now on, the longer you wait to take a team out the harder it is. These guys will get momentum if we don't cut it now."

If the Senators want to keep their Stanley Cup hopes alive, they are going to have to win in New Jersey, where the Devils are 8-0 in these playoffs.

"We don't worry too much about the stats and the past," said rookie Jason Spezza, who had a goal and an assist in sparking Ottawa's win in Game 5. "That's why this team has done so well. We've fought through what everyone's said all year and we're going to try to continue that."

# Devils Get Revenge

**TOM CANAVAN, AP SPORTS WRITER**

EAST RUTHERFORD, N.J.—It might be time to consider the New Jersey Devils a legitimate contender again.

Not only are the Devils winning and scoring, they're even beating the team that embarrassed them in the playoffs last season—the Carolina Hurricanes.

Patrik Elias scored twice, and the streaking New Jersey Devils matched their season high with three power-play goals in beating the Hurricanes 5-2 on Saturday night.

"Getting back-to-back wins against a team that had our number is a great accomplishment for us," goaltender Martin Brodeur said after his second win over the Hurricanes in 24 hours. "We knew we had struggled against them, so we really bore down."

Michael Rupp, John Madden and Turner Stevenson also scored as the Devils extended their season-high unbeaten streak to seven games (6-0-1).

| FINAL | 1st | 2nd | 3rd | T |
|---|---|---|---|---|
| Carolina | 1 | 1 | 0 | 2 |
| New Jersey | 0 | 2 | 3 | 5 |

"We've been looking to streak a little more," said Brodeur, who faced 20 shots. "We're doing the little things to win games. We're scoring more goals."

During their current run, the Devils have scored 26 goals and allowed only 11. They have also improved on special teams. Besides converting on three of eight power-play chances, the Devils killed off all five Carolina power plays.

Elias has been a major contributor. After being limited to one goal in 19 games, he has scored seven in his last eight, including the game winner at 7:52 of the third period.

Elias credits the spurt to finally feeling comfortable skating with Scott Gomez and Jiri Bicek. In previous years, he was with Petr Sykora and Jason Arnott. They were both traded in the last year.

AP/WWP

"I was anticipating plays, but the chemistry wasn't there," Elias said. "I got away from working hard enough. After 25 games, I just started working harder and started getting more and more chances. Now the puck is going in."

The game winner was somewhat lucky.

Defenseman Ken Daneyko took a shot from the left point, and Hurricanes defenseman Aaron Ward tried to kick the puck to the corner. It went right to Elias for a shot into an open net at 7:52 of the third period with goalie Kevin Weekes on the other side of the net.

"It was 2-2 in the third period and we basically shot ourselves," Weekes said. "It's frustating. We know the other side and we know we can and should be a lot better."

Kevyn Adams and Erik Cole scored for Carolina, winless in seven games (0-5-1-1). The defending Eastern Conference-champion Hurricanes are 1-8-1-1 in their last 11.

Madden extended the advantage to 4-2 by putting in the rebound of Colin White's shot at 12:07. Stevenson added an empty-net goal with 15.7 seconds to play.

A scuffle broke out between Sergei Brylin of the Devils and Bret Hedican of Carolina after the goal, but order was quickly restored.

Rupp, who scored twice in his NHL debut on Monday, tied the game at two with 13 seconds left in the second period with the Devils holding a two-man advantage. Stevenson took a point-blank shot that deflected off Rupp's skate.

Cole gave the Hurricanes a 2-1 lead with a great effort midway through the period. He powered his way through Scott Niedermayer's check at the blue line, patiently waited for a sliding Madden to get out of the way, and then ripped the puck past Brodeur.

# January Results

| | | | |
|---|---|---|---|
| Wed. Jan. 1 | Panthers | L 1-2 | 20-11-2-3 |
| Fri. Jan. 3 | Maple Leafs | W 2-0 | 21-11-2-3 |
| Sat. Jan. 4 | at Maple Leafs | L 1-2 | 21-12-2-3 |
| Tue. Jan. 7 | Canadiens | W 3-2 | 22-12-2-3 |
| Fri. Jan. 10 | at Panthers | W 2-1 | 23-12-2-3 |
| Sat. Jan. 11 | at Lightning | T 3-3 | 23-12-3-3 |
| Mon. Jan. 13 | Panthers | W 6-2 | 24-12-3-3 |
| Wed. Jan. 15 | Islanders | W 5-0 | 25-12-3-3 |
| Fri. Jan. 17 | at Hurricanes | W 2-1 | 26-12-3-3 |
| Sat. Jan. 18 | Hurricanes | W 5-2 | 27-12-3-3 |
| Wed. Jan. 22 | at Sharks | W 5-4 | 28-12-3-3 |
| Fri. Jan. 24 | at Mighty Ducks | W 3-1 | 29-12-3-3 |
| Sat. Jan. 25 | at Kings | OTL 1-2 | 29-12-3-4 |
| Tue. Jan. 28 | Red Wings | W 1-0 | 30-12-3-4 |
| Thu. Jan. 30 | Flyers | W 5-1 | 31-12-3-4 |

# JAY PANDOLFO

NO. 20 • HEIGHT 6'1 • WEIGHT 190 • POSITION LW • SHOOTS LEFT • BORN DECEMBER 27, 1974 • BORN WINCHESTER, MASSACHUSETTS

## PANDOLFO'S PRODUCTION NOT GOING UNSUNG FOR DEVILS

JOHN WAWROW, AP SPORTS WRITER

OTTAWA—The way Jay Pandolfo is producing, the New Jersey forward might have to consider relinquishing his title as the Devils' unsung hero.

Pandolfo, whose teammates awarded him the unheralded honor after the regular season, is enjoying the best playoff performance of his career. His surprising offensive touch helped the Devils grab a commanding lead in the Eastern Conference finals.

That advantage was narrowed a bit Monday night when the Ottawa Senators held Pandolfo scoreless and beat the Devils 3-1. New Jersey still leads the best-of-seven series 3-2 and will have Game 6 on home ice Wednesday night.

Not only has Pandolfo been essential in helping contain the Senators' top offensive threats, he also led the Devils with three goals and five points in the series.

"I guess you'd have to take the 'un' out of [unsung]," Devils center Scott Gomez said of his roommate. "We always knew he had it. And it's coming for him, and at no better time than right now."

Pandolfo's emergence has been one of the key reasons the Devils were on the brink of advancing to the Stanley Cup finals for the third time in four years, and fourth time in franchise history.

Long considered one of New Jersey's top defensive specialists, Pandolfo is a plus-nine in the playoffs despite playing against opposing teams' best lines. After helping shut down Boston's Joe Thornton and Tampa Bay's Vincent Lecavalier in the first two rounds, Pandolfo is doing the same against Ottawa's Marian Hossa, who's been limited to one assist.

What's surprising are Pandolfo's offensive contributions, playing alongside center John Madden and right wing Jamie Langenbrunner.

Pandolfo has four goals and nine points in 15 games this postseason, almost doubling the two goals and 14 points he had in his previous 70 playoff appearances.

More important is how timely his production has been.

In New Jersey's 4-1 victory in Game 2, Pandolfo set up Madden's goal to give the Devils a 3-1 lead, then sealed it with a goal in the third period. In Saturday's 5-2 victory, Madden set up Pandolfo to cap a two-on-one short-handed breakaway that tied the game at two.

And Pandolfo should've had a fifth goal when officials failed to detect he had scored—the puck sneaked into a padded liner inside the net and then quickly bounced out—in New Jersey's 1-0 victory over Ottawa in Game 3.

"I don't really feel like I'm playing that much different," Pandolfo said. "I just think that, for whatever reason, the puck's going in for me right now."

He then joked that the goals might be coming because opposing teams never considered him a threat.

"Obviously, I don't think they're going to key on our line to shut us down," Pandolfo said.

Someone should, considering he and his linemates have accounted for five of the Devils' 13 goals in the series.

And it's not as if Pandolfo is foreign to scoring.

At Boston University, Pandolfo had a Hockey East-leading 38 goals as a senior in the 1995-96 season and was a finalist for the Hobey Baker Award given to college hockey's top player.

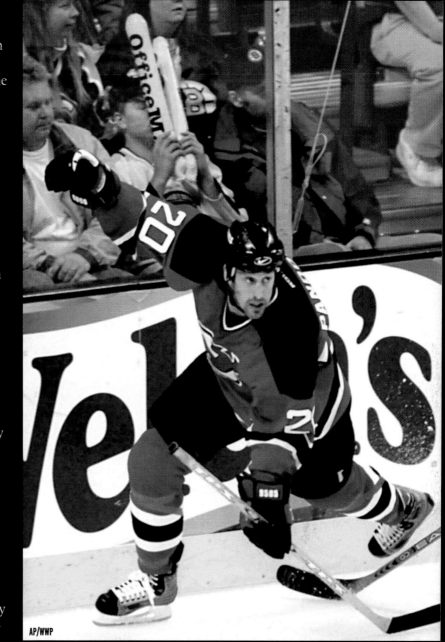

AP/WWP

He traded offense for defense in order to stick with the defensive-minded Devils when breaking into the NHL the following year.

"If there's anybody in this whole dressing room that deserves the glory of scoring goals, it would be Jay," coach Pat Burns said. "He's just a hard

Patrik Elias, who led the Devils in scoring in the regular season, credited confidence as the difference he sees in Pandolfo.

"It's huge when you feel like you can do stuff, and I can see it in him," Elias said. "He's trying to get open and trying to stay in position. He's getting

# Brodeur Notches Seventh Shutout

MEL REISNER, AP SPORTS WRITER

PHOENIX—A rookie mistake that turned out well and a steely veteran in goal were enough for the New Jersey Devils.

Martin Brodeur had 18 saves for his seventh shutout this season and 62nd of his career as the Devils defeated the Phoenix Coyotes 3-0 Wednesday night.

Brodeur (31-16-3) edged closer to his seventh consecutive 35-win season. No other goalie has had more than three straight.

He got the goal he needed when rookie Mike Rupp forgot his shift assignment, caught Phoenix by surprise when he belatedly jumped onto the ice, and scored the tie-breaking goal late in the second period.

"I guess I was thinking," Rupp said. "That was the problem. I shouldn't have been thinking. I just got confused which lines were up."

Added coach Pat Burns: "I looked down, and he's right on the bench. I said, 'Rupper, get out there.' I didn't really see the goal, but he was caught napping on the bench."

| FINAL | 1st | 2nd | 3rd | T |
|---|---|---|---|---|
| New Jersey | 0 | 1 | 2 | 3 |
| Phoenix | 0 | 0 | 0 | 0 |

Jiri Bicek and Jeff Friesen scored in the third period.

The Devils broke out of a short slump with their 35th victory, matching Ottawa for most in the NHL and remaining one point behind the Senators for the top playoff seed in the Eastern Conference.

New Jersey had lost two of three after a 12-0-1-1 run ended, and Brodeur was in net for a 3-1 loss at Colorado the night before.

"We kind of beat ourselves," he said. "They're a hot team, but we just put on our work boots today and worked really hard, stayed disciplined and followed our game plan."

Brian Boucher had 35 saves for the Coyotes, who had difficulty getting past the neutral zone throughout the game and failed to put a shot on net the first half of the third period.

"I thought we had some poor individual efforts tonight," Coyotes coach Bob Francis said. "I don't think we were awful, but I tend to look at individual performances right now, and with some guys I was disappointed in their effort, to be quite honest."

Phoenix has lost four straight and five of its last six.

Branko Radivojevic took Phoenix's 15th shot with 7:30 to go after a short-handed breakaway. It prevented the Coyotes from matching their season-low in attempts; Brodeur kicked it away.

The 30-year-old veteran kept the Coyotes off balance with deep clearing passes after his saves, sometimes into the neutral zone and once to the other end when he didn't like the setup in front of him.

Phoenix's shortcomings were exposed in its two first-period power plays.

The Coyotes failed to get a shot off against the No. 1 defensive club in the NHL, and Boucher had to face three by New Jersey after short-handed rushes by Jamie Langenbrunner and John Madden.

"They are solid up and down, and when they have a breakdown, they have Brodeur to make the big saves, and that's the sign of a great team," Boucher said.

Rupp, playing in his 12th NHL game, broke through against Boucher when his seasoned teammates couldn't, lifting a backhander over the goalie's left shoulder with 4:15 left in the second period. Rupp split Coyotes defenseman Deron Quint and center Daniel Briere with his late entry into the shift, and Jim McKenzie spotted him perfectly for a dash down the slot.

He was cool approaching the net, though.

"I thought the only thing to do was go to the backhand, because I noticed early in the game that Boucher was going down on a lot of shots," he said. "I was just kind of waiting for him to make a move. I still don't know if he did, but I ran out of time, so I had to shoot."

# February Results

| Tue. Feb. 4 | Sabres | W 4-1 | 32-12-3-4 |
|---|---|---|---|
| Wed. Feb. 5 | at Capitals | W 4-1 | 33-12-3-4 |
| Fri. Feb. 7 | Thrashers | L 2-4 | 33-13-3-4 |
| Sun. Feb. 9 | Wild | W 3-2 | 34-13-3-4 |
| Tue. Feb. 11 | at Avalanche | L 1-3 | 34-14-3-4 |
| Wed. Feb. 12 | at Coyotes | W 3-0 | 35-14-3-4 |
| Sat. Feb. 15 | Penguins | L 1-4 | 35-15-3-4 |
| Tue. Feb. 18 | at Flyers | T 2-2 | 35-15-4-4 |
| Wed. Feb. 19 | Senators | L 3-5 | 35-16-4-4 |
| Fri. Feb. 21 | Bruins | W 3-2 | 36-16-4-4 |
| Sun. Feb. 23 | at Penguins | W 4-3 | 37-16-4-4 |
| Tue. Feb. 25 | Rangers | T 3-3 | 37-16-5-4 |
| Thu. Feb. 27 | at Islanders | T 3-3 | 37-16-6-4 |

# SERGEI BRYLIN

NO. 18 • HEIGHT 5'10 • WEIGHT 190 • POSITION C • SHOOTS LEFT • BORN JANUARY 13, 1974 • BORN MOSCOW, U.S.S.R

## BRYLIN RETURNING FROM BROKEN WRIST

TOM CANAVAN, AP SPORTS WRITER

WEST ORANGE, N.J.—Sergei Brylin will be back in the New Jersey Devils' lineup Thursday night against the Tampa Bay Lightning in Game 1 of the Eastern Conference semifinals.

It is the forward's first game since Feb. 5, when he broke his wrist in a game against the Washington Capitals. Brylin had surgery, then couldn't do anything for nearly two months because doctors were afraid of infection.

He missed the last 30 games of the regular season and the first-round playoff victory over Boston.

"I just wanted to play this year," said Brylin, a member of the Devils' Stanley Cup championship teams in 1995 and 2000. "I put a lot of hard work and effort into my rehab and tried to push myself as hard as I could."

He's one of those little cogs that make the Devils tough to beat. He plays on a checking line, kills penalties and can score a big goal

when needed. He had a goal and an assist in New Jersey's championship-clinching game against Detroit in 1995.

"Sergei has been a key part of our team over the years—the unsung hero," defenseman Ken Daneyko said. "We've managed to get this far with him being injured, so to bring in a guy who can play at both ends of the rink is a spark for us. He's a playoff-type player who can only help if he's healthy."

Brylin said he felt fine after practice Tuesday.

"After missing 11 weeks, the only way to find out is to go out and try it," Brylin said.

It was not immediately clear whose place he would take Thursday. Turner Stevenson played well in Brylin's spot on a line with John Madden and Jay Pandolfo.

"He's fast. He's smart. He checks well and contributes on offense," said Madden, whose line will probably be assigned to shut down

the Lightning top line of Vincent Lecavalier, Vaclav Prospal and Martin St. Louis. "That's what makes my job easier. Sergei does it as well as I do. It's great having two guys on the same line like that."

Brylin has also skated with Scott Gomez and Patrik Elias this season, but Brian Gionta and that pair played well together late in the season. The other option would be to put

Brylin on the fourth line, taking one of the wing spots now played by Grant Marshall or Jim McKenzie.

Brylin said his wrist is still a little stiff and not as strong as he would like.

"But it feels better and better every day," Brylin said. "A week ago I wasn't able to do this and that."

# Brodeur Posts Fourth 40-Win in a Row

TOM CANAVAN, AP SPORTS WRITER

EAST RUTHERFORD, N.J.—On a day when Patrik Elias scored four goals and Scott Gomez had five assists, the teammates yielded the spotlight to Martin Brodeur.

| FINAL | 1st | 2nd | 3rd | T |
|---|---|---|---|---|
| NY Islanders | 0 | 0 | 0 | 0 |
| New Jersey | 2 | 1 | 3 | 6 |

Brodeur became the first NHL goaltender to post four 40-win seasons as the New Jersey Devils beat the New York Islanders 6-0 Sunday.

"Consistency is something that when I started my career I wanted to do," said Brodeur, who earlier this year became the first goaltender to record eight consecutive 30-win seasons. "I wanted to be able to play a lot and be consistent every year. Winning so many games every year shows I was able to do that. I want to keep going and raise that bar for other goalies coming up."

Brodeur only had to make 19 saves in recording a league-high ninth shutout this season and the 64th of his career. It improved his record this season to 40-22-8, surpassing Jacques Plante and Terry Sawchuk in career 40-win seasons.

"Sometimes we kind of expect it, because he's so laid back about it all," Gomez said of Brodeur. "But he's special. One of these days I'll be able to tell my grandkids that I played with Marty Brodeur and it will be a wonderful thing to look back on."

Neither Elias nor Gomez will likely forget this game.

Elias's four goals were a career best, and his five points—he also had an assist—tied his previous high. Gomez's five assists tied a team record.

"The last 10 or 15 games, I have been feeling pretty good out there," said Elias, who has 10 of his 27 goals in the last 13 games. "Gomer is playing better and we're working strong as a line."

Scott Stevens and Turner Stevenson also scored, and Joe Nieuwendyk got his 500th career assist as the Devils extended their unbeaten streak to seven games (5-0-2).

The win moved New Jersey four points ahead of the idle Philadelphia Flyers in the Atlantic Division

and within four points of Ottawa in the race for the best record in the Eastern Conference.

The loss was the second straight for the Islanders, who seem to be losing their grip on the eighth and final playoff berth in the Eastern Conference despite being four points ahead of the New York Rangers.

The teams will meet on Tuesday night at the Nassau Coliseum, and that game might be very interesting if the Rangers beat Atlanta on Monday night to move within two points of eighth place.

An angry Michael Peca said the Islanders can't wait until Tuesday to change things.

"We have to see tomorrow, not Tuesday," the Islanders captain said. "We have to see signs when we leave this locker room that no one has accepted this game. I think too often [recently] we've had tough games and haven't shown up, and it's gotten too easy to accept it and move forward to the next one."

The Islanders have two more wins than the

Rangers and would have the first tiebreaker should the teams finished tied.

Elias and Gomez helped give Brodeur the only goal he would need, setting up Stevens in front of Islanders goaltender Rick DiPietro at 5:04 of the first period.

Elias got his first two goals in the second period and two more in the third as New Jersey beat the Islanders for the fourth time in five games (4-0-1).

Elias got his first at 11:52 of the second period, deflecting a Scott Niedermayer shot on a power play. He put in his own rebound after being set up by Gomez in a four-on-four situation.

Elias got the hat trick in the opening minute of the third period on a great setup in front by Brian Gionta, and he added his 27th of the season by poking a puck past DiPietro at 14:11.

Elias's hat trick was the sixth of his career, tying John MacLean for the team record. It was his first four-goal game, and fourth by a Devil. John Madden, Randy McKay and Pat Verbeek were the others.

## March Results

| Sat. Mar. 1 | Capitals | W 2-1 | 38-16-6-4 |
|---|---|---|---|
| Tue. Mar. 4 | at Wild | L 2-3 | 38-17-6-4 |
| Wed. Mar. 5 | at Flames | OTL 4-5 | 38-17-6-5 |
| Sat. Mar. 8 | at Islanders | W 4-2 | 39-17-6-5 |
| Tue. Mar. 11 | Thrashers | L 2-3 | 39-18-6-5 |
| Thu. Mar. 13 | at Bruins | L 3-4 | 39-19-6-5 |
| Sat. Mar. 15 | Rangers | W 3-1 | 40-19-6-5 |
| Mon. Mar. 17 | Flyers | L 2-4 | 40-20-6-5 |
| Tue. Mar. 18 | at Canadiens | W 1-0 | 41-20-6-5 |
| Fri. Mar. 21 | Penguins | W 3-1 | 42-20-6-5 |
| Sat. Mar. 22 | at Islanders | W 4-2 | 43-20-6-5 |
| Mon. Mar. 24 | at Panthers | W 4-1 | 44-20-6-5 |
| Thu. Mar. 27 | at Lightning | T 2-2 | 44-20-7-5 |
| Fri. Mar. 28 | at Thrashers | T 1-1 | 44-20-8-5 |
| Sun. Mar. 30 | Islanders | W 6-0 | 45-20-8-5 |

"I wanted to be able to play a lot and **be consistent** every year. Winning so many games every year shows I was able to do that. I want to **keep going and raise that bar** for other goalies coming up."

—MARTIN BRODEUR

# SCOTT GOMEZ

NO. 23 • HEIGHT 5'11 • WEIGHT 200 • POSITION C • SHOOTS LEFT • BORN DECEMBER 23, 1979 • BORN ANCHORAGE, ALASKA

## AN EMBARRASSED GOMEZ PLAYING HIS BEST HOCKEY

TOM CANAVAN, AP SPORTS WRITER

EAST RUTHERFORD, N.J.—Scott Gomez still has a difficult time giving New Jersey Devils coach Pat Burns credit for jump-starting his game in time for the playoffs.

The 23-year-old center skates around the topic awkwardly before admitting that Burns did him a major favor by benching him before a game against Atlanta last month.

Gomez had three goals and 11 assists in the 14 final regular-season games, and the line of Gomez, Patrik Elias and Brian Gionta might be the Devils' best heading into Wednesday night's Game 1 of their best-of-seven, first-round playoff series with the Boston Bruins.

"Numbers don't lie," Gomez said of his recent surge. "It's just one of those things. You have to give credit where credit is due. We had our ups and downs, and maybe he [Burns] saw the big picture and I was being stubborn about it at first."

Infuriated and embarrassed are better descriptions of how Gomez felt after Burns benched him on March 11.

Not only did Burns keep Gomez out of the lineup that night, the coach didn't bother to tell the four-year veteran.

When Gomez showed up at the Continental Airlines Arena that night, his jersey wasn't hanging in his locker.

In hockey terms, it means you're not playing. It was only the second time all season he missed a game, and the first time he was a healthy scratch.

An annoyed Gomez left the arena before the game ended.

"I never really had someone push a button that made me angry, and maybe that was the thing the whole time," Gomez said. "After that happened, there definitely was a change, an eye opener. That could be the ultimate embarrassment when you are not playing."

To this day, Gomez and Burns have never discussed the incident, Gomez said.

Burns scoffs when asked about the situation.

"I am about as bouncy as a hunk of clay," Burns said. "That's the way I do things. Like me or not, that has no fizz on my mind at all. What's important to me is the progress of the team and the outcome."

The Atlantic Division champions, the Devils played well in the final weeks of the season. They got at least one point in their final 11 regular-season games, including a 1-1 tie with Boston last week.

The Bruins, the seventh seed in the Eastern Conference, finished 3-3-3 in the nine games after Mike O'Connell replaced Robbie Ftorek as coach.

New Jersey was 2-1-1 against the Bruins this season.

"They capitalize on your mistakes," O'Connell said. "They don't make many themselves. So we have to try to do the same. I think our games have been very even, and I think that when you play New Jersey they're very comfortable playing a 0-0 game. They do a very good job at it and we have to do our best to make sure that we're a patient team as well."

While the Bruins may have a little more potent attack with the line of Joe Thornton, Glen Murray and Mike Knuble, New Jersey has an advantage in goal with Martin Brodeur, who led the league in wins and shutouts.

"Marty has won games for us all year long, and he is one of the best in the league right now," Burns said. "I think a goaltender can bring you a long way. He's like a pitcher in baseball. But if nobody hits, it's not worth much. You have to have guys who are hitting."

Neither the Devils nor the Bruins had good opening rounds a year ago.

New Jersey was eliminated in six games by Carolina despite giving up only nine goals in the series. The Bruins, who were the top seed in the Eastern Conference, were stunned by Montreal in six games.

"We had a bad experience in the playoffs, and I think people have that in the backs of their minds," Brodeur said. "We want to avoid that again, just like the Boston Bruins. They probably have the same attitude as us. Mentally, it is going to be hard."

AP/WWP

# Devils Clinch Playoff Spot

**IRA PODELL, AP SPORTS WRITER**

N EW YORK—The New York Rangers' season of promise ended with another guarantee and another spring without a trip to the playoffs.

The Rangers were beaten 2-1 Friday night by the defensively superior New Jersey Devils, who eliminated New York but were happier about clinching the Atlantic Division in the process.

"Winning our division, that's what we had at stake," said Joe Nieuwendyk, who assisted on the winning goal one night after being struck by a puck in the face. "We played a solid team game."

New York general manager and coach Glen Sather, along with team owner James Dolan, guaranteed that the Rangers would make the playoffs this season after a six-year absence, but it wasn't to be.

"It was disappointing," said Sather, who wouldn't commit to returning as coach next season. Sather made his playoff promise when he assumed the coaching duties from rookie Bryan Trottier 54 games into the season.

| FINAL | 1st | 2nd | 3rd | T |
|-------|-----|-----|-----|---|
| New Jersey | 0 | 2 | 0 | 2 |
| NY Rangers | 0 | 1 | 0 | 1 |

Dolan reaffirmed his confidence that Sather is the man to run the Rangers. Dolan promised that ticket prices will remain the same next season. He also said they will drop 10 percent if the Rangers, who have the league's highest payroll, don't make next year's playoffs.

"I think we all felt it was going to be a tough job getting into the playoffs," Dolan said.

Jeff Friesen had a goal and an assist to lead the Devils. The Rangers' loss allowed the rival New York Islanders to clinch the final playoff berth in the Eastern Conference.

"We had all the desperation we needed," Rangers captain Mark Messier said. "We just got shut down."

The Islanders had two chances to eliminate their New York neighbors, but they tied the Rangers on Tuesday and lost to Detroit on Thursday.

So, the Devils—on a 6-0-3-1 run—did the job for the Islanders, clinching their fifth Atlantic title in seven years.

"There was a lot at stake," Devils goalie Martin Brodeur said. "We definitely responded to the challenge."

Brodeur made 18 saves for his 41st win of the season. At the final buzzer, he raised his arms and pumped his fist toward Devils fans seated behind him.

Friesen snapped a 1-1 tie with 5:06 left in the second period when he took a pass from Nieuwendyk.

The Rangers grabbed a 1-0 lead two minutes into the second when Petr Nedved scored his 26th goal, 48 seconds after Nieuwendyk was called for tripping.

But only 1:45 after the goal, Eric Lindros took the latest in a string of costly penalties, and Scott Niedermayer made the Rangers pay for it. Friesen made a pass to Jamie Langenbrunner, who quickly moved it back the other way to Niedermayer. The defenseman deflected the puck past Mike Dunham.

Lindros, who drew two of the game's first four penalties, was booed throughout by the home crowd, which was frustrated by his 16th straight game without a goal and his constant infractions.

Most of Lindros's high-priced teammates were also booed when they were announced one by one in a postgame ceremony in which they gave their jerseys to fans.

"This one is really disappointing for us," said the 42-year-old Messier, who hasn't decided whether he'll return for his 25th NHL season. "The Ranger fans are behind the team all the time. They expect a lot out of us."

Despite tying Boston on Thursday, the Devils came out as the fresher, more aggressive team. They sent 18 shots on net in the first period and 16 more in the second before finishing with 41. The Rangers had just five shots in the third after recording 14 through 40 minutes.

Tom Poti almost tied it with 5:14 left, but his deflection right in front was gloved by Brodeur. Nedved's hard wrister from Brodeur's left was calmly covered with 3:02 remaining.

The Rangers needed to win their final two games and have the Islanders earn no more than one point in their final two contests to reach the playoffs. But the Rangers lost key home games to Florida, Pittsburgh, and Atlanta—all non-playoff teams—down the stretch, which ultimately sealed their fate.

## April Results

| | | | |
|---|---|---|---|
| Tue. Apr. 1 | Maple Leafs | OTL 2-3 | 45-20-8-6 |
| Thu. Apr. 3 | Bruins | T 1-1 | 45-20-9-6 |
| Fri. Apr. 4 | at Rangers | W 2-1 | 46-20-9-6 |
| Sun. Apr. 6 | at Sabres | T 2-2 | 46-20-10-6 |

AP/WWP

# PLAYOFFS
## ROUND 1
### DEVILS DEFEAT BRUINS, 4-1

# Devils Start Off the Right Way

**TOM CANAVAN, AP SPORTS WRITER**

EAST RUTHERFORD, N.J.—The New Jersey Devils started on the right foot in the playoffs this year, keeping Boston's Joe Thornton in check and getting two goals from Jamie Langenbrunner.

Langenbrunner scored twice, and the Devils limited Thornton to one shot and an assist in a 2-1 victory over the Bruins in the opener of their first-round playoff series Wednesday night.

The Devils knew they would have to contain Thornton (36 goals, 65 assists) to avoid a second straight opening-round exit.

"I thought we contained the big line pretty well," Devils goalie Martin Brodeur said after a 26-save performance. "It got hard at one point when they started shuffling them around a little bit. But you've got to be happy. We played Thornton real well."

Thornton started the game centering for Glen Murray and Mike Knuble, his regular linemates. He switched in the second period and worked with Sergei Samsonov and Marty McInnis, and

| FINAL | 1st | 2nd | 3rd | T |
|-------|-----|-----|-----|---|
| Boston | 0 | 0 | 1 | 1 |
| New Jersey | 1 | 1 | 0 | 2 |

played with both lines in the third period, when he set up Bryan Berard's goal to cut the Devils' lead to 2-1.

"We tried to throw them off, but they reacted pretty good," said Thornton, who played 22 minutes, 36 seconds. "We'll just see what happens tomorrow."

Game 2 of the best-of-seven series is Friday night, before the series shifts to Boston for the next two games.

In the opener, Langenbrunner started making amends for a dreadful first-round playoff series last year, when the Devils were eliminated in six games by Carolina.

Acquired along with Joe Nieuwendyk last March in a major trading deadline deal with Dallas, Langenbrunner had one assist in five games.

"I was awful," Langenbrunner said. "I didn't do what I was supposed to do. There was some disappointment in that. I think this year, you want to come in and make up for it. None of us had the playoff we wanted to last year. You don't ever want to lose in the first round. We all have something to prove."

Langenbrunner staked the Devils to a 2-0 lead with goals in each of the first two periods against Steve Shields, who made 26 saves, including a spectacular skate save on John Madden with the net open in the second period.

Langenbrunner gave the Devils the lead with 4:25 left in the first period, beating Shields off a rebound. Langenbrunner stretched the Devils' lead to 2-0 on a bad play by Bruins forward Michal Grosek. His cross-ice pass from deep in his zone hit Nieuwendyk's stick and set up Langenbrunner all alone for a shot from between the circles at 11:38.

"Jamie's played well all year long," Devils coach Pat Burns said. "He does have a knack of getting the big goal at the right time. That goal, when he picked off that pass in the middle, that was heads-up hockey on his part."

After Berard scored early in the third period, Brodeur made three good saves down the stretch to preserve the win. Brodeur made a stick save on Jozef Stumpel on a two-on-one with 8:35 left. The star goalie made a stick and blocker save on Glen Murray a little more than a minute later and he stopped a bouncing shot by Berard with 2:35 to go.

The save on Murray was a little lucky.

"It hit my [stick] knob and blocker and stayed in front of me," Brodeur said after his 68th career playoff win.

The Bruins, stunned by Montreal in the first round of the playoffs a year ago, weren't upset with the way they played.

"I thought we had the upper hand in the third period," Berard said. "We played a lot down in their end and used our size. We made a couple of mistakes that cost us, but it was a good effort."

Berard's goal at 3:28 of the third period was a little controversial because he appeared offside on the play as he took a pass from Thornton.

ROUND 1, GAME 2 | APRIL 11, 2003

# Devils Go Up 2-0 on Bruins

**TOM CANAVAN, AP SPORTS WRITER**

EAST RUTHERFORD, N.J.—After searching all season for a power play, the New Jersey Devils found one in the playoffs.

Jamie Langenbrunner broke a third-period tie with the Devils' second postseason power-play goal as New Jersey beat Boston 4-2 Friday night to take a 2-0 lead in the first-round playoff series.

"It's funny how things work," said Devils center Joe Nieuwendyk, who added an insurance goal later in the third period. "I know the power play is a sore spot for us. It certainly came up big for us tonight."

New Jersey finished last in the league with the extra man this season, and is two of 10 against the Bruins.

Langenbrunner's third goal of the series came with the Devils skating four-on-three. He one-timed Scott Nidermayer's pass to break a 2-2 tie 15 seconds into the final period.

"It was a great play by Nieds to slow it down," said Langenbrunner, who has five points in the series

| FINAL | 1st | 2nd | 3rd | T |
|---|---|---|---|---|
| Boston | 1 | 1 | 0 | 2 |
| New Jersey | 2 | 0 | 2 | 4 |

after getting just one in the Devils' first-round loss to Carolina last year. "I just got myself to the middle of the ice. I got pretty good wood on it and was able to find the hole."

Jeff Friesen, Brian Rafalski and Nieuwendyk also scored, and Martin Brodeur made 24 saves as the Devils became the only team in the first three days of the playoffs to win twice at home.

Glen Murray and Dan McGillis scored for Boston, which will return home for Games 3 and 4 in the best-of-seven series. The Bruins will need a big comeback to avoid a second straight first-round exit.

"Obviously we're not playing good enough," Bruins defenseman Bryan Berard said. "It's frustrating. We just have to get better. It seems every mistake the puck ends up in our net."

The go-ahead goal was another mistake, a slashing

AP/WWP

"There's still time," Bruins captain Joe Thornton said. "We've played well at home all year so we have to play well at home now."

The Bruins again will face a goaltending decision. Steve Shields stopped 26 of 30 shots, but he wasn't as impressive as he was in Game 1, when Langenbrunner was again the difference, scoring twice in a 2-1 game.

Jeff Hackett, who hasn't played in a month because of broken finger, dressed as the Bruins backup Friday.

penalty by defenseman Nick Boynton at the end of the second period.

That put New Jersey on the power play and they didn't need long to deflate the Bruins, who were outshot 11-5 in the final 20 minutes.

"I cost the team," Boynton said. "We should have won that game. I took a dumb penalty and that's that. It was an iffy call."

Brodeur and Rafalski made the lead stand up with big saves on the Bruins' fifth and last power plays.

Brodeur made a great pad save on Murray's shot from between the circles with 8:09 to play. Seconds later, Marty McInnis ripped a shot that fluttered past Brodeur and hit off Rafalski, but the defenseman used his stick to pull the puck away from the net.

"I made the save and it went right off Ralfy's pants," Brodeur said. "I was going to try to whack it, but it hit off Ralfy's shaft and went wide. It's nice when guys are helping out like that."

Langenbrunner iced the game by setting up Nieuwendyk on a breakaway with 5:36 to go.

Boston used a physical game to get the early lead.

Murray hit Scott Stevens behind the Devils net, and New Jersey was forced to send the puck around the boards. Bruins defenseman Ian Moran one-timed a shot on net, and Brodeur stopped Thornton's rebound. Murray scored on the rebound at 8:52.

The Devils seemingly didn't wake up until Stevens made an open-ice hit on Mike Knuble during a Boston power play. Shortly after the penalty ended, Langenbrunner set up Friesen in the left circle with 5:43 left in the period.

Rafalski put the Devils ahead 2-1 with a power-play goal with 26 seconds left in the opening period. The defenseman's shot appeared to hit off a Bruins player on the way in. It came 10 seconds after Knuble was called for interference.

McGillis tied the game, but the Devils took control in the third period after Langenbrunner scored on the power play.

"We just have to win," Bruins forward Michal Grosek said. "We're going to go home and win two games and it will be 2-2."

# Devils a Win Away from Second Round

**HOWARD ULMAN, AP SPORTS WRITER**

BOSTON—Martin Brodeur's latest shutout has the New Jersey Devils a win away from the second round and the Boston Bruins wondering how to get the puck past him.

| FINAL | 1st | 2nd | 3rd | T |
|---|---|---|---|---|
| New Jersey | 0 | 1 | 2 | 3 |
| Boston | 0 | 0 | 0 | 0 |

Brodeur posted his 14th shutout in 70 career playoff wins Sunday when the Devils beat the Bruins 3-0 for a 3-0 lead in their best-of-seven, first-round series.

"They have, basically, an unbelievable wall back there and that weighs on you," Boston's Mike Knuble said.

It should bother New Jersey's potential playoff opponents, especially with the confidence and sense of near-invincibility that Brodeur brings to the playoffs.

"I still have a long way to go and many more shutouts to get," he said.

New Jersey can sweep Tuesday night in Boston and send the Bruins to another first-round exit. Seeded first in the Eastern Conference last year, they lost in six games to Montreal.

Now they face a daunting task. In the 13 series in which they have trailed 3-0, the Bruins have never made it to a sixth game. They lost seven of those series 4-0 and six 4-1.

"Anything's doable," said Boston's Brian Rolston, who managed just one shot Sunday and has no points in the series.

The Devils got goals from Scott Stevens in the second period, Jay Pandolfo in the third and John Madden into an empty net with 1:06 left.

The Bruins got none of their 29 shots past Brodeur, who led the league with 41 wins and nine shutouts and was fourth with a 2.02 goals-against average.

"He's a big-time goalie and thrives on games like this," Madden said. "He plays just well enough to be better than everybody, but when big games come he takes it to another level."

Last season, the Devils lost in the first round in six games to Carolina, which reached the Stanley Cup finals. It was a big disappointment to a team that won the championship in 2000 and lost in the finals in 2001.

"Last year, we weren't 100 percent [healthy] going in," Stevens said. "We just look at this as another year."

This season, New Jersey tied Philadelphia for the fewest goals allowed. And the Devils don't rely on a single line as much as the Bruins do.

"Every time we get in their end it seems like they dump it out and we have to come back, regroup and then get back in," said Joe Thornton, Boston's first-line center. "They're a patient team."

Boston goalie Jeff Hackett, who missed the previous 12 games since breaking his right index finger March 15, played well and saved 19 of 21 shots. He started in place of Steve Shields, who played in the 2-1 and 4-2 losses in the first two games.

"I felt good," Hackett said, but "sometimes one goal is too much against New Jersey."

All the offense Brodeur needed was Stevens's 24th career playoff goal and first this year at 1:11 of the second period.

Stevens shot from the left point into a crowd. Boston defenseman Ian Moran inadvertently pushed Hackett toward the left side, and the puck sailed by the goalie's right side.

"I didn't see the puck," Hackett said.

Pandolfo made it 2-0 at 12:00 of the third when he flipped the puck over a diving Hackett. Madden assisted on both goals

At 7:04 of the second period, defenseman Dan McGillis blocked a puck at his own blue line and broke in alone. He shot from 10 feet, but

Brodeur blocked the puck with his left shoulder and caught it in his left hand before tumbling backward in his crease.

Brodeur frustrated the Bruins again early in the third period. He stopped P. J. Axelsson's shot from the right circle with his right pad and the rebound went to his left.

"I thought Axelsson had me on the first shot, but I reacted quickly and got lucky," Brodeur said.

Axelsson took another shot, but Brodeur slid across the crease to catch it with his left glove at 1:50.

"That was probably the save of the game," Devils coach Pat Burns said.

The Bruins started aggressively in a well-played first period. But they were called for the first four penalties of the game, including two against Michal Grosek for interfering with Brodeur.

But the Devils had the NHL's worst power play in the regular season and were 0 for five with the extra man Sunday.

AP/WWP

# Bruins Say "Not So Fast"

**HOWARD ULMAN, AP SPORTS WRITER**

BOSTON—The Boston Bruins didn't suddenly discover a secret plan to get the puck past Martin Brodeur. The plan they'd been using all along finally worked.

| FINAL | 1st | 2nd | 3rd | T |
|---|---|---|---|---|
| New Jersey | 0 | 0 | 1 | 1 |
| Boston | 1 | 1 | 2 | 5 |

Pepper him with shots. Create traffic in front of the crease. Pounce on rebounds.

The Bruins did all that for the fourth straight game Tuesday night and finally beat New Jersey. The 5-1 victory kept them in the NHL playoffs, trailing 3-1 in the best-of-seven series going into Thursday night's game at the Devils' home.

"It was no different tonight," Bruins coach Mike O'Connell said. "I'd like to tell you that I made all these changes to score these goals, but that wasn't the case."

For once, the puck seemed to take the right hop onto a Boston player's stick and get by Brodeur while his vision was blocked by other players.

Boston got the critical first goal, forcing the defense-oriented Devils to open up their game to try to catch up. Joe Thornton scored off a rebound on a power play with 13 seconds left in the first period.

"They had the good bounces going for them," Devils coach Pat Burns said. The puck "came right back on Joe's stick."

Then Boston capitalized on another rebound as Dan McGillis made it 2-0 on a power play at 2:24 of the second period. He converted from 15 feet after Jonathan Girard's shot ricocheted off Brodeur's left shoulder.

McGillis, who had just three goals in 71 regular-season games, scored his second of the game and third of the playoffs at 17:15 of the second period, making it 3-0.

"We thought we played pretty good hockey" in the first three games, he said. "We're playing close games against a stingy defense with a great

goaltender and we had some opportunities and missed."

They connected on Tuesday against the same goalie who stopped 79 of 82 shots in the first three games. In the fourth game, he turned aside only 19 of 24 before being replaced by Corey Schwab after Marty McInnis made it 5-1 at 3:37 of the third period.

"We weren't happy with the way we played," Brodeur said, "but the fact is, when the series started, we'd have taken 3-1 going back to our building in a heartbeat."

On Tuesday, Boston's Jeff Hackett was the best goalie. He lost his shutout on Scott Niedermayer's first goal of the playoffs at 1:37 of the third period.

But goals by Martin Lapointe and McInnis in the next two minutes gave Boston the momentum again.

"It didn't bother me at all to get out of there and get some rest," Brodeur said. "They know I'm human. Hopefully, they'll take different kinds of shots than the perfect shots they took tonight."

The Bruins, who have won just one playoff series in the last eight years, are more confident as they try to become only the third team in NHL history to win a series after trailing 3-0.

"If we lost four straight it would have been very embarrassing," Hackett said. "It would have been almost as bad as not making the playoffs."

**ROUND 1, GAME 5 | APRIL 17, 2003**

# Devils Eliminate Bruins

TOM CANAVAN, AP SPORTS WRITER

EAST RUTHERFORD, N.J.—John Madden shut down Joe Thornton and silenced the critics in helping the New Jersey Devils eliminate Boston in the first round of the Stanley Cup playoffs.

The little center put an exclamation point on a spectacular series Thursday night by scoring a goal and setting up two others by Jamie Langenbrunner as the Devils beat the Bruins 3-0 in Game 5.

The second-seeded Devils will play either Tampa Bay, Philadelphia or Toronto in the second round, but the opponent won't be determined until early next week.

There were some who felt the seventh-seeded Bruins had a chance to upset the Devils because they felt Madden would not be able to handle Thornton, who is five inches taller and 30 pounds heavier.

Madden more than held his own. He limited the young Boston star to a goal and two assists, while leading the Devils with two goals and six assists for eight points.

| FINAL | 1st | 2nd | 3rd | T |
|-------|-----|-----|-----|---|
| Boston | 0 | 0 | 0 | 0 |
| New Jersey | 1 | 0 | 2 | 3 |

"He played well," Thornton said after the Bruins were eliminated in the first round for the second straight year.

Madden declined to take all the credit.

"No one guy is going to shut down Joe Thornton or their line," Madden said. "It took a lot of guys."

Defensemen Scott Stevens and Brian Rafalski were on the ice almost every time Thornton stepped out, and Madden was joined by linemates Jay Pandolfo and Turner Stevenson.

However, Madden added that he was annoyed by the comments about his size being a problem.

"I think his whole life he's been told he's too small and that he can't do things," Stevens said. "He's determined and he works hard. I read a quote in

"Marty was fabulous," Devils coach Pat Burns said. "He took a little bit of heat. He's a pro's pro, a true professional. We saw it again tonight. He stood up and came right back."

Bruins coach and general manager Mike O'Connell, who replaced Robbie Ftorek as coach late in the season, will head into the off season with a lot of things to think about.

"Did I have the time to do the necessary things? Probably not," O'Connell said. "You're put in the position that I accept as a general manager and you have to make some difficult decisions.

"Did I get all the bases covered? No, but I think I addressed some of the issues that needed to be addressed."

The Bruins weren't as smart as the Devils when it came to competing in the postseason. It was apparent in the final game, when Boston picked up five consecutive penalties.

his stall that he had stuck up about that. He was definitely motivated. He's a smart player. He's capable of shutting down people."

If Thornton and company found ways to get by Madden, they still had to contend with Martin Brodeur.

Brodeur only gave up three goals in the Devils' four wins. His lone bad outing came in a 5-1 loss in Game 4 on Tuesday night, a game he finished on the bench.

Brodeur didn't take long to bounce back, making 28 saves in the series-winning game and recording his second shutout of the series and 15th of his career.

Madden gave New Jersey the lead at 8:31 of the first period, converting the first power-play chance with a shot that beat a screened Jeff Hackett, who played well, making 28 saves.

Langenbrunner, who led Devils with five goals in the series, converted Madden's pass in close at 7:41 of the third period for a 2-0 lead and added an empty-net goal in the final minute.

"It's huge for us to get a couple of days off," said Langenbrunner, who had only one point in the Devils' first-round loss last year. "We won the series 4-1, but this was a battle. They played physical and hard. It took a lot for us to get the wins, so the days off will be great for us."

# PLAYOFFS
## ROUND 2
### DEVILS DEFEAT LIGHTNING, 4-1

# Lightning Scoreless in Game One

**IRA PODELL, AP SPORTS WRITER**

EAST RUTHERFORD, N.J.—The sight of Scott Stevens being knocked to the ice was so stunning that everything seemed to stop.

Everything except Jamie Langenbrunner.

Langenbrunner had a goal and an assist 3:47 apart in the third period, and Martin Brodeur made 15 saves in his third shutout of these playoffs as the New Jersey Devils beat the Tampa Bay Lightning 3-0 Thursday night.

After Stevens, the Devils' hard-hitting defenseman, was leveled by a shoulder check from Vincent Lecavalier in the neutral zone, Langenbrunner got the puck and skated over the blue line on his way to making it 1-0.

"I saw those guys collide at center ice and I just took off with the puck," Langenbrunner said.

Langenbrunner was guarded by defenseman Pavel Kubina when he let a shot go that dipped on its way from above the left circle and got through Nikolai Khabibulin's legs as the goalie shifted 7:41 into the third.

| FINAL | 1st | 2nd | 3rd | T |
|---|---|---|---|---|
| Tampa Bay | 0 | 0 | 0 | 0 |
| New Jersey | 0 | 0 | 3 | 3 |

"I was as surprised as anyone that it was in the net," said Langenbrunner, who had five goals and seven points in the first round. "I pride myself in playing well in big games."

Game 2 of the best-of-seven series is Saturday. The Lightning will be looking for a better effort in their first appearance in the conference semifinals in 11 years of existence.

Stevens shook off the check he absorbed, both on the ice and after the game.

"It wasn't hard at all; he just caught a piece of me," he said.

Not long after that, he sent Langenbrunner streaking down the ice again.

A shot clanked off Stevens's leg in front of Brodeur, and he swept the puck right to Langenbrunner as he skated down right wing. John Madden criss-

crossed behind him, took a drop pass, and ripped a shot past Khabibulin for Madden's third goal of the playoffs. Madden had a team-high eight points in the first round.

"I think we can play better. You can always play better," Madden said.

Brodeur and the Devils eliminated Boston in the first round with a 3-0 victory in Game 5. They made it back-to-back blankings with a stellar defensive effort, the fifth time Brodeur had consecutive playoff shutouts.

"It's important that we establish ourselves," Brodeur said. "It's not going to be an easy series for them. They'll have to work hard to try and beat us. We have a good system and we've got to play it well. In the first game we showed them how we're going to play."

Turner Stevenson scored with 2:50 left on New Jersey's 31st shot, further sealing Brodeur's 16th postseason shutout. The most he ever had in one playoff year was four in 2001.

"We're not going to win versus this team if Marty has to make one save a game and their defense plays great," Lightning forward Dave Andreychuk said.

The pre-series talk was about top goalies Brodeur and Khabibulin. Neither allowed a goal through two periods, mostly because so few pucks came their way.

Martin St. Louis and the rest of the Lightning quickly lost the scoring touch that led them to four straight first-round victories after dropping the first two games. St. Louis scored the game winner

in the final three games against Washington, but had his four-game goal streak snapped by the Devils.

"There's a fine line between being patient and just sitting back," he said. "I thought we gave them way too much respect. We didn't play physical, we didn't finish checks, we didn't make it tough on them."

Khabibulin looked shaky fighting off the six shots that reached him in the first period. He either kicked out big rebounds that were cleared away by teammates, or dropped pucks from his glove that he quickly covered.

The New Jersey power play that clicked only three times in 22 chances in the first round against Boston didn't look any more potent this time, going 0 for three.

Brodeur isn't concerned.

"We're playing playoff hockey," Brodeur said. "We're playing well enough to survive and we're doing the little things that keep us out of trouble. We take a lot of icings. We take no chances of turning the puck over."

# Woes Continue for Lightning

**IRA PODELL, AP SPORTS WRITER**

EAST RUTHERFORD, N.J.—Jamie Langenbrunner made Vincent Lecavalier's already tough game that much worse.

| FINAL | 1st | 2nd | 3rd | OT | T |
|-------|-----|-----|-----|-----|---|
| Tampa Bay | 1 | 1 | 0 | 0 | 2 |
| New Jersey | 0 | 1 | 1 | 1 | 3 |

Langenbrunner went around the struggling Tampa Bay forward and scored his second straight game winner 2:09 into overtime Saturday as the New Jersey Devils beat the Lightning 3-2.

New Jersey leads the best-of-seven Eastern Conference semifinal series 2-0, with the next two games in Florida. Game 3 is Monday.

Langenbrunner, who has seven goals in seven games this postseason, took a pass from John Madden and fired a shot from the right circle that goalie Nikolai Khabibulin fumbled. Langenbrunner rushed in past Lecavalier for the rebound, made a move around Khabibulin, and slid the puck in.

"I hit a pretty poor shot and hit him right in the chest," Langenbrunner said. "I hit him high enough that it was hard to control it. Coach has been preaching going to the net all week, and fortunately it came right back out to me."

Langenbrunner had 10 playoff goals in 1999 to help Dallas to the Stanley Cup title. He had 25 goals in the regular season for the Devils.

"He's a guy that doesn't stop working," captain Scott Stevens said. "He comes to play every night and he's got a lot of energy. He competes and that's what the playoffs are all about."

Lecavalier is having a tough time generating offense against Madden's checking line. After recording just one shot in Tampa Bay's Game 1 loss, Lecavalier—the team's second leading scorer in the regular season—had no shots Saturday.

But the Lightning have been here before. They lost the first two games of the first round to Washington and then won four straight.

"Against Washington I didn't produce the first two

AP/WWP

games, and after that it went well," Lecavalier said. "Hopefully it's going to be the same way."

The Devils had to rally twice to win this one.

Not long after New Jersey's Martin Brodeur stacked the pads to stop Martin St. Louis's breakaway, Grant Marshall got the Devils even for the second time. Scott Gomez took a shot from the slot that was knocked in by Marshall to make it 2-2 with 9:34 remaining in regulation.

St. Louis's short-handed goal on another breakaway gave the Lightning a 2-1 lead. Brodeur had that in mind when St. Louis came in alone again.

"I wanted him to make the first move," Brodeur said. "When he went to his backhand, I just kind of stacked the pads and made the save.

"When the same guy gets two breakaways, sometimes it gets in your head. I was calm and able to make the save."

Brian Rafalski had the other New Jersey goal.

The Lightning grabbed their first lead of the series with 7:35 left in the first period.

Chris Dingman lightly deflected Dan Boyle's pass through the legs of New Jersey defenseman Scott Niedermayer and past Brodeur for his first playoff goal in 23 career games to make it 1-0.

It snapped Brodeur's shutout streak of 132 minutes, 25 seconds and New Jersey's run of 148:48 without allowing a goal. The Devils weren't scored on since the third period of their Game 4 loss to Boston.

New Jersey got even late in the second period that was dominated by Devils penalties and an ineffective Tampa Bay power play. After taking one penalty in their Game 1 victory, New Jersey was whistled for four in the second.

Having weathered that, the Devils were given their second power play of the game with 2:31 left. It had 22 seconds remaining when Tim Taylor was called for roughing, giving New Jersey a two-man advantage.

The Devils were three for 26 on the power play in these playoffs before cashing in on Rafalski's goal with two seconds left on the first penalty. Rafalski scored with 33.4 seconds left in the period.

Khabibulin stopped the first 22 shots he faced this series, then allowed three goals in the third period of Game 1 on nine shots, before stopping 23 more in a row leading up to Rafalski's goal.

Rafalski, who missed Game 1 due to illness, had two goals. Before his goal was announced, he got burned by St. Louis. The small Lightning forward rushed past Rafalski and scored with 21.7 seconds left in the period.

The Lightning, 0 for five on the power play this series, had eight shots in each of the regulation periods—the same as their third-period total of Game 1 when they had 15 overall.

# Lightning Blaze Back

**FRED GOODALL, AP SPORTS WRITER**

TAMPA, Fla.—The Tampa Bay Lightning blew a big lead, though not an opportunity to climb back into their playoff series with the New Jersey Devils.

The Lightning squandered a three-goal advantage Monday night, but Dave Andreychuk snapped a third-period tie and lifted Tampa Bay to a 4-3 victory over the Devils in Game 3 of the second-round matchup.

Playing with the same sense of urgency that helped them overcome a two-game deficit in the first round, the Lightning now trail the Devils 2-1 as they try to rally in the Eastern Conference semifinals.

"You don't want to script it that way, but you find a way to get it done," Tampa Bay coach John Tortorella said.

"It's another lesson, something we battled through. ... To come back in the third period, keep our patience and find a way, it's something you can draw on when you get in those situations again," he added.

Andreychuk scored the game winner with 13:52 remaining, taking advantage of the Devils being unable to complete a line change that left New

| FINAL | 1st | 2nd | 3rd | T |
|---|---|---|---|---|
| New Jersey | 0 | 3 | 0 | 3 |
| Tampa Bay | 3 | 0 | 1 | 4 |

Jersey with four forwards and just one defenseman in front of goaltender Martin Brodeur.

Devils coach Pat Burns screamed at the officials and pounded on the boards in front of his bench when defenseman Colin White was ordered off the ice.

"After all these years in the league, am I that stupid that I would put four forwards and one defenseman in a 3-3 tie in the third period? I think everybody who knows me here knows I'm not that stupid," Burns said.

"I might be halfway stupid, but not that stupid. It was the wrong call. ... We played hard and fought back. If we lose the game because they scored a couple of good goals, and they outplayed us, fine. But I just feel bad about losing the game like that."

Nikolai Khabibulin rebounded from a shaky second period to make two key saves in the final two minutes with New Jersey desperately trying to take advantage of a power play.

"It was a do-or-die game for them, and obviously we didn't have that approach," New Jersey's Jeff Friesen said.

The Devils won the first two games of the series at home, but the victory bolstered the Lightning's confidence that they can again rally to prolong their first playoff appearance in seven years.

Game 4 of the best-of-seven series is Wednesday night in Tampa. The series returns to New Jersey for Game 5 on Friday night.

"We're still down 1-2. We've got a game in our building," Andreychuk said. "The pressure is on to win."

New Jersey played most of the game without captain Scott Stevens, who left early in the first period after a shot by Tampa Bay's Pavel Kubina hit him in the left ear, opening a cut that required stitches.

"I think losing Scotty definitely hurt us," Burns said. "I think morale-wise it hurt us a little bit to see the gladiator that he is come off the ice the way he did. I think that really shook the bench up a little bit."

Vinny Prospal, Martin St. Louis and Fredrik Modin scored first-period goals for Tampa Bay, which won four straight to eliminate Washington after losing the first two games at home in the first round.

Prospal scored when his shot deflected into the net off the stick of White just over four minutes in. Five minutes later, St. Louis added his seventh goal of the playoffs for a 2-0 lead.

When Modin scored from the right circle to make it 3-0, it looked bleak for the Devils, who rallied

from one-goal deficits twice before winning Game 2 in overtime. But Brodeur dug in the rest of the way, and New Jersey launched an impressive comeback.

John Madden and Grant Marshall scored less than a minute apart in the second period to trim Tampa Bay's lead to 3-2. Friesen's shot from the left circle, which officials determined was a goal after a video replay, made it 3-3 late in the period.

Andreychuk broke the tie from in front of the net, just moments after Madden nearly beat Khabibulin with a shot that caromed off the right post.

The goal came after the Devils were unable to get the proper personnel on the ice before a faceoff in the Tampa Bay zone. New Jersey won the faceoff and Madden's shot hit the post before the Lightning moved up ice and scored.

Dave Newell, NHL supervisor of officials for the series, said the Devils were slow in getting White onto the ice.

"We can't make exceptions that you only have one defenseman out there," Newell said. "You've had your time to change and these are the five players that are on the ice, and these are the five players that have to play."

# Stevens's Presence Seals Win

**FRED GOODALL, AP SPORTS WRITER**

TAMPA, Fla.—Tough guy Scott Stevens was a tad nervous.

Fortunately for New Jersey, he didn't play that way Wednesday night in helping the Devils take a 3-1 lead in their best-of-seven playoff series against the Tampa Bay Lightning.

Stevens returned to the lineup two nights after being hit in the left ear with a puck and showed just how much he means to the NHL's top defensive team.

Wearing a helmet fitted with extra padding, he scored a goal and was on the ice for all three in a 3-1 victory. The Devils can reach the Eastern Conference finals for the third time in four years by winning Game 5 at home Friday night.

"We did ourselves a big favor by winning, there's no question about that. This is a huge game for us, and we got the job done," Stevens said. "We want to build on it, go back home and play a great game. … If we play like we did tonight, we should have a good chance."

| FINAL | 1st | 2nd | 3rd | T |
|---|---|---|---|---|
| New Jersey | 2 | 0 | 1 | 3 |
| Tampa Bay | 1 | 0 | 0 | 1 |

With Stevens back, the rest of the Devils are confident, too.

"For everybody, to have him back so quick, was definitely a relief," goalie Martin Brodeur said.

"I don't think we needed much of a boost to get ourselves going. It was a big game. But the way he played was excellent."

Stevens missed all but 77 seconds of Game 3 Monday night after Pavel Kubina's slap shot hit him in the side of the face, opening a cut requiring 15 stitches—and adding an element of controversy to the series.

Some of the New Jersey captain's teammates wondered whether Kubina intentionally shot the puck at Stevens, drawing an angry response from Lightning coach John Tortorella and his players.

Kubina denied he was aiming at Stevens and apologized to the 13-time All-Star, who didn't practice Tuesday and wasn't sure he would play in Game 4 until after testing his helmet and taking some bumps from teammates in warmups.

"I was definitely a little nervous," Stevens said. "Our equipment manager did a good job, and the doctors reassured me that things should be fine. But it was my call. No one put pressure on me."

Scott Gomez and Patrik Elias scored first-period goals for New Jersey. Stevens added his second playoff goal on a power play with 6:47 left in the third, giving Brodeur some breathing room down the stretch.

AP/WWP

"He's an unbelievable leader. We need him in the lineup," New Jersey's John Madden said of Stevens, who has played in 138 consecutive playoff games since joining the Devils in 1991.

"He'll go down in the history books as one of the toughest guys ever to play the game. I've seen him endure a lot of things that would make a grown man cry. When he goes in the hockey Hall of Fame, that's one of the things I'll remember about him is his toughness."

The 39-year-old Stevens played more than 10 minutes of the opening period and finished with a team-high 27:35 of ice time. Not bad for a guy who went to bed the night before thinking his chances of playing were slim.

New Jersey coach Pat Burns said he felt all along that Stevens would find a way to be ready.

"That's just the type of individual he is. He played a solid game. ... He didn't play like a guy that was trying to protect an injury. He did everything," Burns said.

Jassen Cullimore scored Tampa Bay's goal, briefly making it 1-1 late in the first period.

The Lightning rallied to win four straight after losing the first two games of its opening-round series against Washington. They know it will be more difficult to come back on one of the league's best defensive teams.

"We know what we're up against. We're fighting hard. We're battling," Tortorella said. "It's such a fine line, winning and losing."

Still, Tampa Bay's players haven't given up hope.

"It's tough," defenseman Dan Boyle said, "but not impossible."

# Devils Take Series in Triple OT

TOM CANAVAN, AP SPORTS WRITER

EAST RUTHERFORD, N.J.—Grant Marshall made up for nearly missing the team bus by taking the New Jersey Devils to the Eastern Conference finals for the third time in four years.

Marshall scored on a rebound at 11:12 of the third overtime, and the Devils eliminated the Tampa Bay Lightning with a 2-1 victory in Game 5 on Friday night.

The Devils will face the winner of the Philadelphia-Ottawa series for the right to advance to the Stanley Cup finals. The Flyers and Senators are tied 2-2 in their best-of-seven series.

Marshall, who scored three goals in the series, was waiting for the bus to leave for the game when he went to get a drink.

"I still had 15 minutes, so I thought I had plenty of time," Marshall said. "I glanced out and the bus was pulling away. I had to run out to get the bus and [coach] Pat [Burns] was joking saying it wasn't him."

| FINAL | 1st | 2nd | 3rd | OT | 2OT | 3OT | T |
|---|---|---|---|---|---|---|---|
| Tampa Bay | 1 | 0 | 0 | 0 | 0 | 0 | 1 |
| New Jersey | 1 | 0 | 0 | 0 | 0 | 1 | 2 |

Marshall was in the right spot in the third overtime to send the Devils to their fourth appearance in the conference finals since 1995.

Scott Niedermayer, who scored the Devils' other goal, took a shot from above the right circle into a crowd in front of the goal.

Niedermayer thought his shot deflected off Marshall into Lightning goalie John Grahame, who was spectacular, making 46 saves in a surprise start for Nikolai Khabibulin.

The puck fell at Marshall's feet and he backhanded it into the net.

"I just kept whacking at it," Marshall said. "I just stepped and fired it five-hole. My goals aren't the prettiest, but as long as I can have one that's great. During the intermission, I was thinking how great it would be to get a game winner."

The Devils have not lost a conference final since 1994 against the Rangers. They have won two Stanley Cups and lost a third in a deciding Game 7 to Colorado in 2001.

"We're only halfway there, but the way things are going in the NHL this year, you never know," Devils captain Scott Stevens said. "We took a big step tonight winning this game."

Martin Brodeur, who allowed just eight goals in the five games against the Lightning, made 38 saves in the second longest game in Devils history.

Nikita Alexeev scored for the Lightning, who reached the conference semifinals for the first time in their 11-year existence.

"You don't want this to be a one-time thing and rest on your laurels," Lightning coach John Tortorella said. "You have to keep on building. You don't want a one-year thing. I know we had fun playing in the playoffs and we'd like to come back next year."

Tampa Bay rallied from an 0-2 series deficit to beat Washington in the opening round, but never threatened New Jersey after losing the first two games in this series.

"A game like that, it's great when you win and devastating when you lose," Grahame said.

Grahame and Brodeur both had big saves in the overtime periods to keep the game going.

Grahame, who never appeared in the postseason and hadn't played since the final game of the regular season, stopped John Madden on a point-blank rebound of Jamie Langenbrunner's shot with 8:23 to go in the first overtime. He also stopped a shot in close by Brian Gionta.

In the second overtime, Grahame stopped Langenbrunner with a shoulder save and made an armpit save on Scott Gomez.

Brodeur stopped Martin St. Louis in close in the third period after being hit in the facemask by a shot by Brad Richards. Brodeur also had a nice pad save on Alexeev minutes later.

Brodeur also had good stops on Ruslan Fedotenko and St. Louis in the first overtime.

"They played well," Brodeur said. "They had no tomorrow and they played a solid game and their goalie was awesome. We kept shooting pucks at the net and got rewarded."

Alexeev gave the Lightning the lead at 11:18, beating Brodeur on a two-on-one break after Niedermayer got caught deep in the Tampa Bay zone.

Niedermayer made up for the mistake a little more than two minutes later, scoring in close on a power play. The Devils seemingly got away with a couple of penalties just before the goal.

Gomez sent Dave Andreychuk to the ice with a tug, and Marshall knocked defenseman Cory Sarich off balance. That allowed Niedermayer to get the puck inside the circles for a shot that beat Grahame along the ice.

Modin, who was in the penalty box when Niedermayer scored, thought he gave the Lightning a 2-1 lead with 8:18 left in the second period on a rebound in close.

However, the goal was disallowed when video replays showed Modin kicked the puck into the net—although the Lightning could have argued Modin was hit from behind, forcing his leg forward.

# PLAYOFFS
## ROUND 3
### DEVILS DEFEAT SENATORS, 4-3

**ROUND 3, GAME 1 | MAY 10, 2003**

# Senators Win Game 1 in OT

**JOHN WAWROW, AP SPORTS WRITER**

OTTAWA—The Ottawa Senators weren't kidding when they boasted about their depth on offense.

Checking-line forward Shaun Van Allen tipped Martin Havlat's pass into a wide-open net 3:08 into overtime Saturday night, leading the Senators to a 3-2 victory over the New Jersey Devils in the opening game of the Eastern Conference finals.

Van Allen's first career goal in 55 playoff games came after the Senators squandered an early 2-0 lead.

Chris Neil and Todd White also scored for the Senators, whose more potent scorers—including Marian Hossa and captain Daniel Alfredsson—were held without a point. Patrick Lalime finished with 32 saves and set a playoff record with his 11th straight game of allowing two goals or fewer.

Joe Nieuwendyk and Jay Pandolfo scored for the Devils, and Martin Brodeur made 27 saves.

"I'm still tingling," Van Allen said. "It's been a long time in the making, and it was a big goal, but my linemates deserve a lot of credit."

| FINAL | 1st | 2nd | 3rd | OT | T |
|---|---|---|---|---|---|
| New Jersey | 0 | 2 | 0 | 0 | 2 |
| Ottawa | 2 | 0 | 0 | 1 | 3 |

Peter Schaefer sparked the game-winning goal, forcing a turnover and feeding Van Allen to set up a two-on-one break. Van Allen fed a pass across, drawing Brodeur to the top of the crease, and Havlat sent the puck back to Van Allen.

"You've got the whole net there, and you just have to redirect it," Van Allen said. "Anyone's going to score that goal."

Game 2 of the best-of-seven series is at Ottawa on Tuesday.

While the Devils showed determination in rallying from a two-goal deficit, they couldn't overtake the Presidents' Trophy winners.

And in making their deepest playoff run, the Senators continue erasing memories of past early-round exits, including last year when they squandered a 3-2 second-round series lead against Toronto.

"We've been learning through the years," Lalime said. "Adversity, the last few years, we've had some good playoffs, but not as good as this. And now we start to believe we can do it, and that's probably the difference this year."

The Senators haven't lost a playoff game this year in which they've scored. Ottawa was shut out once by the New York Islanders and twice by Philadelphia in the first two rounds.

The Devils, making their third Eastern Conference finals appearance in four years, aren't worried yet.

"I don't think anybody's going to panic in this locker room," Nieuwendyk said. "It sure would've been nice to get this one after coming back. But they're a good hockey club over there."

The Senators improved to 9-3 in the playoffs, while New Jersey lost its first Game 1 this year and fell to 8-3. The Devils eliminated Boston and Tampa Bay in five games in the first two rounds.

AP/WWP

The Senators appeared to be in control when they scored twice on their first four shots 7:23 in.

Magnus Arvedson's blind backhander toward the net deflected in off Neil's skate. White scored 73 seconds later by flipping in a rebound after Brodeur kicked away Chris Phillips's point shot.

The Devils, playing their first game since May 2, responded with a pair of goals 2:32 apart in the second period, capped by Pandolfo's one-timer from the top of the left circle.

In a series involving this postseason's two best goalies, Lalime had the early edge—stopping the first 19 shots he faced. He got his blocker out to deflect Brian Gionta's shot from in close in the early going.

Brodeur was strong in keeping the Devils in it. Along with stopping Bryan Smolinski on a two-on-one break late in the first period, Brodeur foiled Alfredsson on a breakaway, getting his stick out to prevent him from cutting across the slot.

His best save came 4:30 into the third against Havlat, who was in alone. Faking forehand, Havlat went backhand only to have his shot stopped when Brodeur held his ground and kicked out his left leg.

New Jersey's Scott Niedermayer left the game shortly before the winning goal. The defenseman appeared woozy and required help getting off the ice after he was struck in the back of the helmet by a point shot from Ottawa's Anton Volchenkov.

Niedermayer said he sustained a bruise, but doesn't expect to be held out of action.

# Devils Battle Back to Even Series

JOHN WAWROW, AP SPORTS WRITER

OTTAWA—The New Jersey Devils might have the Ottawa Senators' attention now.

After spending the past few days hearing about how deep in talent the Senators were, the Devils mustered a significant response.

Martin Brodeur stopped 30 shots, and New Jersey's offense came up with a big effort as the Devils beat the Senators 4-1 on Tuesday night to even their NHL Eastern Conference finals series.

John Madden, Tommy Albelin, Jeff Friesen and Jay Pandolfo scored for the Devils, who erased questions whether they can contain the potent Senators and bounce back from Saturday's sloppy series-opening 3-2 overtime loss.

"They are a good hockey club, but so are we," Devils coach Pat Burns said. "But we didn't come in here through luck like everybody said."

The Devils, making their third conference finals appearance in four years, also seemed stung by the perceived lack of respect they got from their opponents after the opener.

| FINAL | 1st | 2nd | 3rd | T |
|-------|-----|-----|-----|---|
| New Jersey | 2 | 0 | 2 | 4 |
| Ottawa | 0 | 1 | 0 | 1 |

"They were awfully excited winning Game 1," Devils center Joe Nieuwendyk said. "But there's a lot of guys that have been through these long battles before, and it takes four to win a series."

In the Western Conference final, Minnesota is at Anaheim on Wednesday night with the Mighty Ducks leading the series 2-0.

It's the Senators' turn to respond as the best-of-seven series, tied at 1-1, shifts to New Jersey, where the Devils are 6-0 during the playoffs.

"Who cares?" Senators forward Bryan Smolinski said, referring to the Devils' unbeaten home record. "It doesn't matter. We're still a fantastic team."

The Senators, who finished with NHL's best regular-season record, didn't look so fantastic in Game 2.

They came out flat, generated few scoring chances, finished 0 for seven in power-play opportunities, and allowed more than two goals for the first time in 12 games, ending an NHL playoff record streak they set in Game 1.

Smolinski did credit the Devils for how they responded.

The loss was also the Senators' first in which they've scored this postseason. They were shut out in their three previous losses, once against the New York Islanders, and twice by Philadelphia.

After jumping out to a 2-0 first-period lead, the Devils put the game away after Ottawa's Radek Bonk scored early in the second period.

Madden beat Senators defenseman Karel Rachunek to a loose puck to score on a partial break at the 16:33 mark of the second, and Pandolfo's goal sealed the win with 5:31 left.

"It was looking pretty bleak from everybody after we lost the first game," Devils captain Scott Stevens said. "But we felt we wanted to come and get this game tonight. We battled hard and got a big team effort from everyone."

The Senators might have to continue without defenseman Wade Redden, who was favoring his right knee and didn't return after he left midway through the third because of a knee-on-knee collision with New Jersey's Turner Stevenson.

Senators coach Jacques Martin said Redden was still being evaluated.

Ottawa defenseman Curtis Leschyshyn accused Stevenson of sticking his leg out.

"It's not going over big right now," Leschyshyn said. "You can't be sticking your knee out, accidentally or not."

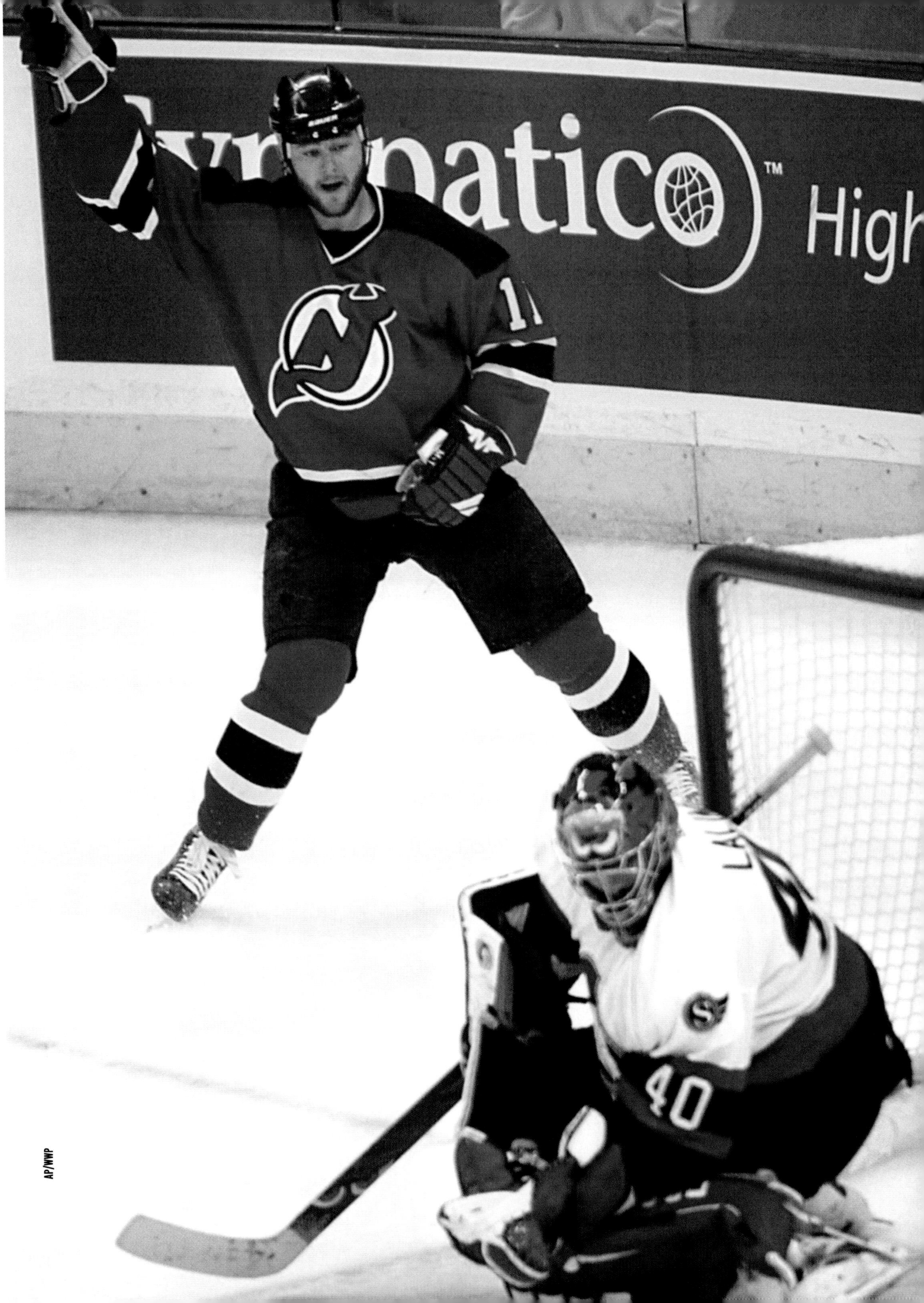


AP/WWP

# Devils Hang On to Beat Senators

TOM CANAVAN, AP SPORTS WRITER

EAST RUTHERFORD, N.J.—Martin Brodeur and the New Jersey Devils took the NHL off the hook—and put Ottawa on it.

| FINAL | 1st | 2nd | 3rd | T |
|---|---|---|---|---|
| Ottawa | 0 | 0 | 0 | 0 |
| New Jersey | 1 | 0 | 0 | 1 |

Brodeur made 24 saves for his fourth shutout of the playoffs and Sergei Brylin scored the only goal the league deemed to count in a 1-0 victory Thursday night. The Devils lead the Eastern Conference finals 2-1, with Game 4 set for Saturday at the Meadowlands.

Game 3 will remembered for the goal the NHL missed with New Jersey leading 1-0 with 7:50 left in the first period.

Jay Pandolfo took a pass from Jamie Langenbrunner and slid a shot under Senators goalie Patrick Lalime.

"I could have sworn I saw it go through his legs," Pandolfo said.

A not-so-funny thing happened, though.

Goal judge Paul McInnis didn't put on the red light. Referee Kerry Fraser didn't signal a goal, and the Devils didn't celebrate, other than Langenbrunner raising his stick briefly as he skated around the net.

"I guess I'll start celebrating every shot now," Langenbrunner said, laughing.

After replays officials didn't see anything on the first few replays, the game resumed with a hurry-up faceoff.

Some 40 seconds later, the replay officials got an in-net camera view, which was their third option following the overhead net angle and television replays. The angle showed the puck going into the net, hitting the roll inside it and bouncing back out quickly, ending up under Lalime.

The discovery came too late for the Devils. Because play had re-started, the error could not be corrected.

neutral zone. The Senators had only 11 shots on goal in the first two periods in losing consecutive games for the first time in the playoffs.

When they finally got untracked in the third period and fired 13 shots on goal, Brodeur handled every one.

"Marty has come up big for us all year long, and tonight was no different," Devils defenseman Colin White said. "That's what makes him such a great performer: the playoffs. That's when his true colors come out."

The only puck that really fooled Brodeur was a first-period dump in from center ice by Bryan Smolinski about five minutes after the opening faceoff.

Brodeur went behind the net to play the puck after it hit off the glass in the corner, but the puck took an unbelievable bounce and rolled right through the crease, missing the wide-open net by inches.

"I couldn't believe it didn't go in," said Brodeur, who shook his head behind the net as the puck rolled harmlessly to the corner. "Sometimes you need breaks like that."

Brylin scored at 10:48 of the first period, just seconds after he was tripped carrying the puck in the left circle. Senators defenseman Karel Rachunek retrieved the loose puck behind the net and tried to clear it around the side boards.

Devils defenseman Brian Rafalski stopped the puck at the point and fired a low shot that Brylin tipped into the net with his back to Lalime.

Ottawa had about five or six good scoring chances, with the best being a third-period shot by Radek Bonk that Brodeur made a snapping glove save.

"In this case, it didn't affect the outcome of the game," said NHL executive vice president Colin Campbell in admitting the league erred on the play. "But we can't let it happen again."

To the Devils' credit, they didn't get caught up in the mistake, which came to their attention in the final minutes of the period when the replay was shown on a big screen inside the arena.

Devils coach Pat Burns waved his arms in disgust after watching it.

However, the team's veterans took control between periods.

"We just said let's move on and forget about it," captain Scott Stevens said after New Jersey pushed its home record in the playoffs to 7-0. "Fortunately everything worked out and we won the game."

New Jersey moved within two games of reaching the Stanley Cup finals for the third time in four years by bottling up Ottawa's swift offense in the

PLAYOFFS

# Pandolfo Nets Biggest Goal of the Season

IRA PODELL, AP SPORTS WRITER

EAST RUTHERFORD, N.J.—The next time the New Jersey Devils put their undefeated home mark on the line, they hope it'll be in the Stanley Cup finals.

The Devils took a major step closer to their third finals appearance in four years Saturday with a three-goal outburst in the third period of a 5-2 victory over the Ottawa Senators.

Jeff Friesen, Patrik Elias and John Madden scored in the first 7:35 of the final period to break open a tie game and give the No. 2 seeded Devils a 3-1 lead in the best-of-seven Eastern Conference finals.

New Jersey is 8-0 at home in the postseason and can advance to the finals against the West champion Anaheim Mighty Ducks with a win Monday at Ottawa.

"We have to be ready for our best game," Friesen said.

No one, except maybe Scott Niedermayer, is looking ahead to a matchup with the Ducks.

| FINAL | 1st | 2nd | 3rd | T |
|---|---|---|---|---|
| Ottawa | 1 | 1 | 0 | 2 |
| New Jersey | 1 | 1 | 3 | 5 |

"They're the best team in the NHL," forward Scott Gomez said of Ottawa. "To think about Anaheim would be crazy, absolutely crazy."

But that's what these playoffs have been all along, especially out West. The seventh-seeded Mighty Ducks knocked out the top two seeds—Dallas and Detroit—before completing a sweep of equally surprising Minnesota on Friday in the conference finals.

Ottawa earned the top seed in the East after accruing an NHL-best 113 points.

The Senators looked every bit like that team in the first two periods, when they held a 23-13 shots advantage. New Jersey scored on its first shot 7:25 in, before Karel Rachunek and Vaclav Varada put Ottawa on top.

"This is a game we didn't dominate, but we found a way to win," Friesen said. "We got timely goals, and obviously Jay Pandolfo's goal was the biggest goal of the season."

Pandolfo tied it late in the second period.

"I'm glad they didn't take that one back," said Pandolfo, who lost a goal that wasn't detected two days earlier.

Niedermayer, a two-time champion, is one New Jersey player who can't help but have his thoughts wander a bit. His brother Rob is an Anaheim forward, and the pair would become the first opposing brothers in the Stanley Cup finals since 1946.

"Of course you think about it," he said. "But I don't think about it too much. We still have more work to do."

Niedermayer didn't talk to his brother since Anaheim completed a sweep of Minnesota on Friday. He planned to call him later Saturday.

"I'm just excited for him," he said. "I've had opportunities in the past, and that's pretty much how I look at it now."

Pandolfo has three goals in this series and should have four. He was denied that goal in Game 3 when play resumed following a stoppage, but before replays showed the puck entered the net. The NHL admitted the error, but too late.

It didn't matter as the Devils won 1-0 to grab the lead in the series in which they dropped the opener. On Saturday, Martin Brodeur made 26 saves.

The Senators have dropped a season-worst three straight games. They also had two three-game losing streaks in the regular season.

And now the club that shook off bankruptcy and late paychecks is close to failing to reach its first Stanley Cup finals in its 11-year history.

Ottawa forward Daniel Alfredsson, limited to just one point in the series, took a roughing penalty in the offensive zone with 51.7 seconds left in the middle period.

The Devils converted 41 seconds into the third when Brian Rafalski's drive was deflected by Friesen between Patrick Lalime's pads to make it 3-2.

It was the second power-play goal of the game for the Devils, who failed on their first 12 man advantages of the series. Alfredsson took two penalties that led to New Jersey goals.

"Any time you take penalties you feel responsible. Those were weak calls," Alfredsson said.

Elias, the Devils' leading scorer this season, made it 4-2 with just his second goal of the playoffs. Then Madden scored a short-handed goal.

Alfredsson assisted on Rachunek's goal, which tied it 1-1 with 14.5 seconds left in the first period. Alfredsson was second on the club with 79 points in the regular season, but had none in the first three games.

Ottawa's top scorer, Marian Hossa, also has just one assist in the series.

"We have thrived spreading the scoring out. Those guys are key guys, but as a team we have to pull through," forward Mike Fisher said.

The Senators got even when Alfredsson took advantage of a Devils turnover and set up Rachunek's spin-around goal from the blue line. The goal snapped Brodeur's shutout streak at 117 minutes, 43 seconds.

It was just reward for the Senators, who outshot the Devils 11- 3.

# Senators Cut Series Lead

TOM CANAVAN, AP SPORTS WRITER

OTTAWA—Jason Spezza used a stellar playoff debut to keep the Ottawa Senators' unprecedented run alive.

The 19-year-old rookie scored a goal and set up Martin Havlat's game winner in Ottawa's 3-1 victory over the New Jersey Devils in the Eastern Conference finals on Monday.

The victory not only cut the Devils' series lead to 3-2, it snapped Ottawa's three-game losing streak and forced Game 6 at New Jersey on Wednesday. It also marked the first time in seven tries the Senators won when facing elimination.

Spezza, who had just a few hours to prepare for his first postseason game, had difficulty realizing what he helped accomplish.

"I'm just happy to be here playing with this group of guys," he said.

Spezza's teammates were more than capable of providing perspective, even though the Senators are in the conference finals for the first time in their 11-year history.

| FINAL | 1st | 2nd | 3rd | T |
|-------|-----|-----|-----|---|
| New Jersey | 0 | 1 | 0 | 1 |
| Ottawa | 0 | 1 | 2 | 3 |

"I'm sure he was nervous, but he didn't look nervous. He looked very poised," forward Bryan Smolinski said. "I'm sure all of Canada's talking about him right now. And he deserves every bit of it."

Added captain Daniel Alfredsson: "It is a very tough situation to come in, and he handled it real well."

The Senators still have a lot of work left if they are going to reach to the Stanley Cup finals for the first time.

"We stepped up and got one," defenseman Chris Phillips said. "It was a huge win for us and a big momentum lift. But there's still two more to go."

The series winner will next face the Anaheim Mighty Ducks, who are resting after completing a sweep of the Minnesota Wild in the West finals.

The Devils, attempting to reach the Stanley Cup finals for the third time in four years, are certainly aware of the situation. They don't intend to let the Senators off the hook again.

"They still have to win two more to win the series," said captain Scott Stevens, who scored the Devils' goal. "So we have to regroup and play a better game than we did here. But the ball's in our court."

It helps that the Devils are 8-0 in these playoffs at home and have never lost a series when leading 3-1.

"We're not panicking here," goaltender Martin Brodeur said. "I think it's a little setback. ... But now it's over and we've got to bear down and play better."

Spezza, selected second overall by Ottawa in the 2001 draft, provided the Senators' sluggish offense an immediate lift after it was limited in three previous games.

Four minutes after Havlat put the Senators up 2-1 by capping a scramble in front, Spezza sealed the victory by redirecting Phillips's hard pass into the slot with 7:32 remaining. It was Ottawa's first power-play goal of the series, following an 0-for-20 streak.

Havlat's goal was a strange one. Brodeur made the initial stop, preventing Havlat from jamming the puck in. Brodeur then blindly kicked the puck away, when it hit the skate of New Jersey defenseman Richard Smehlik and rolled back into the net.

Todd White also scored for the Senators.

"This is big for us," said Spezza, who replaced tough guy Chris Neil in the lineup. "We're only getting started now, and we've got a long way to go. But obviously it feels good to help contribute."

Just don't ask Devils coach Pat Burns to rate Spezza's performance.

# Ottawa Evens Series

**IRA PODELL, AP SPORTS WRITER**

EAST RUTHERFORD, N.J.—The Ottawa Senators were short on cash in the regular season. Now they're rich with momentum in the Eastern Conference finals.

| FINAL | 1st | 2nd | 3rd | OT | T |
|---|---|---|---|---|---|
| Ottawa | 0 | 1 | 0 | 1 | 2 |
| New Jersey | 0 | 0 | 1 | 0 | 1 |

Defenseman Chris Phillips scored 15:51 into overtime to lift the Senators to a 2-1 victory Wednesday night and force a Game 7 on Friday in Ottawa. It was the second straight game the Senators fought off elimination.

"Even when we were down 3-1, there was not one guy in our dressing room or organization that counted ourselves out," Phillips said.

Vaclav Varada was trying to hit the loose puck in front of Devils goalie Martin Brodeur, but all he was making contact with was the New Jersey goalie. Trailing the play, Phillips found the loose puck behind Varada and fired it into the net.

"I was just able to get in there and get a whack at it," Phillips said. "I didn't even realize it went in until the other guys started celebrating."

Patrick Lalime kept the Senators alive in the extra session by fighting off several New Jersey flurries. The biggest threat came from Brian Gionta, who was stopped on a 2-on-1 with Patrik Elias.

New Jersey, trying to reach the Stanley Cup finals for the third time in four years, has never lost a series in which it led 3-1. The Senators have never advanced this far in the playoffs in their 11-year history.

"We have to play one game. That's going to be the hardest game," said forward Marian Hossa who assisted on both Ottawa goals. "We're going to be home and that's a good thing."

The West-champion Anaheim Mighty Ducks haven't played since last Friday, but will face the winner on the road in Game 1 of the finals on Tuesday night.

"That's all we wanted to do, to have practice tomorrow," forward Bryan Smolinski said.

There have been 17 comebacks from 3-1 deficits, including three in this year's playoffs.

"We have a big Game 7 ahead of us and we have to start thinking about that," said Joe Nieuwendyk, who scored the Devils' goal.

The Senators, 4-0 in overtime in the postseason, filed for bankruptcy and were late with players' paychecks during the season. Now they have squared the series.

"We like our odds going back home, but we know we are going to have to be better," Senators captain Daniel Alfredsson said. "They are a veteran team that's going to come to Ottawa and play their best."

The Devils were beaten on the road in Game 5 and then sustained their first home loss in this postseason following an 8-0 start. New Jersey sports 15 players who have won the Stanley Cup, compared to only one on the Senators.

"We're a good hockey club when our backs are up against the wall," Devils forward John Madden said. "Sad to say, but that's what it takes sometimes to see the character of this team."

Despite choppy ice that had to be attended to several times during the game, both goalies were sharp. A daytime college graduation held at the arena left holes in the ice in the neutral zone.

In making 30 saves, Lalime looked more like the goalie who held opponents to two goals or fewer in 11 straight playoff games than the one who yielded 10 goals to the Devils in three consecutive losses after Game 1.

Brodeur made 32 saves for New Jersey and has allowed just nine goals in nine home playoff games.

New Jersey, on its first two-game losing streak of the playoffs, tied it in the third period when Wade Redden was off for cross-checking.

On the power play, Scott Niedermayer sent the puck behind the net to Jeff Friesen. He tried to slide the puck in front, but it bounced off Senators defenseman Karel Rachunek, kneeling in front of him.

The puck caromed into the pads of Lalime and out to Nieuwendyk, who slid it back between the

goalie's pads at 2:41 for his 60th playoff goal. The Devils are just three of 21 on the power play in the series.

Nieuwendyk almost scored earlier, but Lalime stopped a breakaway in the second period. Nieuwendyk left the ice with assistance after the game due to an injury sustained in overtime.

Ottawa took a 1-0 lead with a power-play goal. The Senators failed on their first 20 power-play attempts of the series before rookie Jason Spezza scored in Game 5 to seal Ottawa's 3-1 victory on Monday.

The Senators were one for 23 when Radek Bonk put the Senators in front.

Brodeur failed on a clearing attempt, and Hossa worked the puck over to Bonk in the left circle. Bonk sneaked a shot between Brodeur's pads. Both teams had early chances that were turned away either by the goalies or the posts.

Devils defenseman Colin White sent a fluttering shot from the left point that got through and hit the crossbar less than four minutes in. White also took the blame for leaving the front of the net clear on the winning goal.

# Devils Clinch Trip to the Finals

**IRA PODELL, AP SPORTS WRITER**

OTTAWA—Jeff Friesen's first trip to the Stanley Cup finals is taking him home—home to Anaheim.

"It's funny how your career works," said Friesen, dealt to New Jersey last summer from Anaheim.

The New Jersey forward had an eventful third period Friday night, first putting his team in jeopardy and then pushing the Devils a step closer to another championship.

Friesen atoned for an early third-period mistake that cost New Jersey the tying goal by finishing off a pretty passing play that lifted the Devils to a 3-2 victory over the Ottawa Senators in Game 7 of the Eastern Conference finals.

"How fitting, Jeff Friesen turns the puck over and they tie it up," Devils defenseman Ken Daneyko said. "We wanted to kill him, but all of a sudden he becomes the hero."

Friesen spent one full season and part of another with the Mighty Ducks—New Jersey's opponent in its third finals appearance in four years. It

| FINAL | 1st | 2nd | 3rd | T |
|---|---|---|---|---|
| New Jersey | 0 | 2 | 1 | 3 |
| Ottawa | 1 | 0 | 1 | 2 |

wasn't the happiest of times for him in Southern California, but Friesen keeps his off-season home there.

He didn't want to leave the San Jose Sharks, who traded him to Anaheim to get high-scoring forward Teemu Selanne.

"It was a real tough year," Friesen said. "San Jose was a powerhouse, I was traded for Selanne, and that didn't seem to work out."

What did pay off was the deal that landed him in New Jersey. There are 15 Devils who have their names on the Stanley Cup. Friesen isn't one of them.

"It was a big series for us to win, and now we have one more—Anaheim for all the marbles," he said.

His turnover led to Radek Bonk's tying goal at 1:53 of the third period. But words from coach Pat

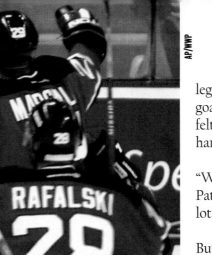

legs and onto Friesen's stick. The goal silenced a frenzied crowd that felt destiny was in their team's hands.

"We battled back," Senators goalie Patrick Lalime said. "We showed a lot of character coming back."

But the Devils are the Eastern Conference champions again. Game 1 against Anaheim is Tuesday night in New Jersey.

It was a bitter ending for the Senators, who overcame bankruptcy, late paychecks and a checkered playoff history in a stirring season.

"Our goal was to go further. It's starting to hit me now," Redden said. "It happened so quick."

Ottawa was the NHL's top team in the regular season, and seemed poised to reach the finals for the first time in its 11-year history. The Senators won Game 5 at home, the first time they ever avoided elimination, and they took Game 6 on the road Wednesday.

Legions of fans, including Canadian Prime Minister Jean Chretien, packed the Corel Centre and were sent into a frenzy when Arvedson scored his first playoff goal.

New Jersey was in danger of losing a series it led 3-1 for the first time. Instead the Devils improved to 5-6 in Game 7s. Ottawa hoped to be the first Canadian team to reach the Stanley Cup finals since Vancouver in 1994.

Burns and several teammates—including injured forward Joe Nieuwendyk—kept him focused.

"I made a bad play at their blue line," Friesen said. "I couldn't believe it, there was a lot going on in my mind."

At that time there weren't too many thoughts that he would score his third game winner of the series.

"I couldn't even describe what that was like," Friesen said. "It just happened to work out that I got a chance."

The Devils, champions in 2000 and finalists in 2001, led the series 3-1 before dropping consecutive games for the first time in the postseason. That got the Presidents' Trophy-winning Senators into a deciding game few thought would occur.

"We weren't disappointed when we came here for Game 7," Friesen said.

Ottawa took a 1-0 lead when Magnus Arvedson scored 3:33 in, but Jamie Langenbrunner scored goals 1:54 apart to put New Jersey in front. After Bonk retied it, Friesen atoned for his error.

Grant Marshall put a perfect pass from the left circle between Ottawa defenseman Wade Redden's

Langenbrunner tied it at 3:52 of the second and then put the Devils in front at 5:46. He was the Devils' biggest offensive force in their first two rounds against Boston and Tampa Bay—both five-game victories—when he scored seven goals.

"What changed it? They went in tonight," Langenbrunner said.

# STANLEY CUP
# FINALS
## DEVILS DEFEAT DUCKS, 4-3

# Devils Take Series Lead

**ALAN ROBINSON, AP SPORTS WRITER**

EAST RUTHERFORD, N.J.—Jeff Friesen wouldn't trade this for anything: a Stanley Cup finals lead against his old team.

Friesen, the very reason the Devils are playing in their third finals in four years, beat former teammate Jean-Sebastien Giguere for the all-important first goal during a two-goal night and the Devils beat the offense-less Anaheim Mighty Ducks 3-0 in Game 1 Tuesday night.

Playing on a makeshift line that was missing injured center Joe Nieuwendyk, Friesen scored his fourth game-winning goal in seven games to halt the momentum Anaheim brought into the finals off stunning upsets of powers Detroit and Dallas and a four-game sweep of Minnesota.

"Playing my old team, that gave me some jump," Friesen said.

Unable to knock the rust off from a 10-day layoff that was the longest ever for a Stanley Cup finalist, Anaheim looked like ducks out of water against the patient, make-no-mistakes Devils, who now take a 1-0 lead into Game 2 Thursday night.

| FINAL | 1st | 2nd | 3rd | T |
|---|---|---|---|---|
| Anaheim | 0 | 0 | 0 | 0 |
| New Jersey | 0 | 1 | 2 | 3 |

"In fairness to them, you could tell they had a little rust on their blades," said Devils coach Pat Burns, coaching in his first finals since 1986. "But they'll get better as the series goes along."

The Ducks gave up only 21 goals in their first 14 playoff games but also scored only 33, and they don't have a single scorer among the top 15 in the playoffs.

That scarcity of offense showed up against a Devils team that allowed the fewest goals in the league during the season; Anaheim had only four shots in each of the first two periods and 16 overall, and so few good scoring chances that goalie Martin Brodeur often went minutes at a time without seeing the puck in his end.

It was Brodeur's first finals shutout, his fifth in this year's playoffs and the 18th overall in his career, second only to Patrick Roy's 23.

AP/WWP

"The shutout isn't important; the win is," Brodeur said. "Now, our magic number is three."

It also was for Friesen, who got three game-winning goals in New Jersey's tense elimination of NHL regular-season champion Ottawa in the Eastern Conference finals—the most in any playoff round since the Islanders' Mike Bossy also had three in 1984. His goal late in Game 7 on Friday night sent New Jersey back to the finals.

Friesen, traded from the Mighty Ducks to the Devils in the deal involving Petr Sykora last summer, added an empty-net goal with 22 seconds remaining, his seventh of the playoffs.

In a game in which the first goal figured to win it in a matchup of the league's hottest goalie (Giguere) against arguably its best goalie (Brodeur), the Devils pressured Giguere from the start.

Finally, Sergei Brylin—substituting for the injured Nieuwendyk on the Devils' second line—controlled the puck near the blue line and swept it to Friesen near the left faceoff circle dot, and he whipped it over Giguere's right shoulder just inside the near post at 1:45 of the second.

"You don't usually think the first one's going to be the game winner, but with Marty, it often is," Friesen said. "Playing with Giguere, I got to know some of his tendencies. He plays just like Patrick Roy; anything you shoot below 18 inches, forget about it."

In not even 22 minutes, the Devils had as many goals as the Minnesota Wild scored against Giguere in the entire Western Conference final. It was only one goal, but the Mighty Ducks, named after a Disney movie, had to sense that the script in this game might be different.

"I felt in the second period the rink was tilted badly; we pressed and then it was here they come," Ducks coach Mike Babcock said. "But we still had an opportunity going into the third period we probably didn't deserve."

The Ducks pulled off the near impossible in their first three series, winning Games 1 and 2 on the road, including multiple-overtime wins in each Game 1. But this night, they asked Giguere to do the truly impossible: win a game for them in which they didn't score.

Giguere, trained by the same goaltending coach who tutored the now-retired Roy, was outstanding most of the game and certainly wasn't the reason the Ducks lost their first finals game ever. They had won only one playoff series before this season.

"I knew it would be tough to generate offense against them," Babcock said. "What I expected was it also would be tough for them to generate offense against us. We had a big opportunity tonight, but we're not going to make excuses. They were hungrier than us."

AP/WWP

And if a 1-0 lead seemed big, the 2-0 advantage supplied by Grant Marshall's fifth playoff goal in 12 games must have seemed insurmountable to the Ducks.

Giguere stopped Patrik Elias's shot from below the right circle, but the rebound deflected back to Elias's stick, and he immediately fed it across the slot to a wide-open Marshall for an uncontested goal at 5:34 of the second.

"Pat stuck with the rebound and that made my job a lot easier," Marshall said.

Marshall went 65 playoff games without a goal, but now has five in his last 12 games.

"He's starting to like it," Burns said.

# Brodeur, Devils Goose-Egg Ducks Again

ALAN ROBINSON, AP SPORTS WRITER

EAST RUTHERFORD, N.J.—The trade that helped get the Anaheim Mighty Ducks into the NHL finals may cost them the Stanley Cup.

Patrik Elias and Scott Gomez scored second-period goals set up by the seldom-used Oleg Tverdovsky and the New Jersey Devils seized a 2-0 lead in the finals with a defense-driven 3-0 victory over the Ducks on Thursday night.

Martin Brodeur tied the just-retired Patrick Roy's record of six shutouts in a playoff year with his second in a row, and just as in a 3-0 victory in Game 1, was barely challenged. The Ducks had only 16 shots, including just two in the Devils' decisive second period, and have only 32 in two games.

Remarkably, the key to the Devils' victory, just as in Game 1, was a player obtained from Anaheim in a trade for Petr Sykora last summer. Jeff Friesen had two goals in Game 1 and another in Game 2.

The Devils, suffocating the Ducks with a trapping defense that gives up shots as grudgingly as some

| FINAL | 1st | 2nd | 3rd | T |
|---|---|---|---|---|
| Anaheim | 0 | 0 | 0 | 0 |
| New Jersey | 0 | 2 | 1 | 3 |

teams give up goals, go to Anaheim for Game 3 on Saturday with a lead that has almost guaranteed the Cup in the past. New Jersey is going for its third Cup since 1995.

Of the 28 teams to sweep Games 1 and 2 at home in the finals, only one—the Chicago Blackhawks, against Montreal in 1971—has not won hockey's biggest prize.

Anaheim's problem right now isn't just winning, but scoring. The Ducks knocked off the rust that was evident in Game 1 following a 10-day layoff and were visibly faster and more physical in Game 2. The trouble was that didn't translate into good scoring chances.

Again, the Ducks' biggest threats—Paul Kariya, Sykora, Adam Oates—were practically invisible. At least on offense.

AP/WWP

Tverdovsky, so deep in coach Pat Burns's doghouse earlier in the playoffs that he was scratched for eight of the last nine games before the finals, created both Devils goals in the second period simply by throwing the puck on the net from the right point.

With the teams scoreless early in the second period, just as they were in Game 1, and Sykora in the penalty box for holding, Tverdovsky's pass caromed off Ducks defenseman Kurt Sauer as he became tangled with Grant Marshall in front of the net and bounced to an unguarded Elias for a tap-in at 4:42.

Before last year's trade, Elias and Sykora formed two-thirds of the 'A' Line, with Jason Arnott, that led the Devils to the Stanley Cup in 2000.

Tverdovsky, scratched in all but one game of the seven-game Eastern Conference finals, was playing mostly because of Burns's hunch that he might be motivated by opposing his former team.

Apparently, he was.

Just over seven minutes later, Tverdovsky again pushed the puck toward the net from the right circle and it deflected off Gomez's knee and past Ducks goalie Jean-Sebastien Giguere for only his second goal in 18 playoff games. His two assists in the period were one-quarter as many as Tverdovsky had in 50 regular season games and doubled his playoff points total.

By now, the rare sellout crowd in Continental Airlines Arena was serenading Giguere with the chant "Marty's better," and, at least for two games, Brodeur has been that.

In the Western Conference finals against Minnesota, Giguere had three consecutive shutouts before allowing one goal in Game 4.

Now it's Brodeur that's got a shutout string going. And if the 2-0 lead wasn't comfortable enough for Brodeur, Friesen added his third of the finals with a seemingly harmless backhander that eluded a screened Giguere at 4:22 of the third.

# Devils Could Use Faceoff Help

**KEN PETERS, AP SPORTS WRITER**

**A**NAHEIM, Calif.—The Mighty Ducks set up the overtime goal in Game 3 by capturing a faceoff. Adam Oates got a clean draw against New Jersey's Pascal Rheaume back to Ruslan Salei for the game-winning wrist shot.

The Ducks held a 51-30 edge in faceoffs in the 3-2 victory Saturday night, but Devils coach Pat Burns indicated help might be on the way for a team that has been one of the NHL's worst in faceoffs all season.

Joe Nieuwendyk, who played only three shifts since injuring a hip in Game 6 of the Eastern Conference finals, is skilled on faceoffs and might be able to play soon.

"We can't invent a top faceoff guy right now going into Game 4 of the finals of the Stanley Cup," Burns said before Monday's game. "Who knows, maybe Nieuwendyk might be suiting up the next game."

Both Nieuwendyk and the Devils have been mum on the exact nature and status of his injury.

| FINAL | 1st | 2nd | 3rd | OT | T |
|-------|-----|-----|-----|-----|---|
| New Jersey | 0 | 1 | 1 | 0 | 2 |
| Anaheim | 0 | 2 | 0 | 1 | 3 |

New Jersey's John Madden believes there's another reason the Ducks have had a big advantage in faceoffs. He claimed they are cheating by gliding in without stopping and not putting their sticks on the ice.

Oates responded by saying, "Maybe he was trying to send a little message, trying to get to the refs."

## Momentum

The Devils mostly laughed and shrugged off goaltender Martin Brodeur's gaffe that allowed Anaheim's second goal in the Ducks' 3-2 overtime win in Game 3.

Some of the Ducks, however, said it was a big deal. Brodeur dropped his stick, and the puck ricocheted off it and into the net to tie it 2-2 in the second period.

Anaheim goalie Jean-Sebastien Giguere said that, despite the Devils' downplaying the mistake, it was a big deal.

The Ducks' Steve Thomas said, "I think momentum in a series could turn on something like that. At least I hope it does."

Predictably, New Jersey coach Pat Burns said there was no lingering effect on his team from the fluke goal.

"It didn't affect us. Giguere can think what he wants. I would worry about his game more than I would worry about Marty's game," Burns said.

Asked if he worries about a fluky goal changing the series, he shot back, "No."

Brodeur was still laughing about the goofy goal.

"I was looking at it on the news," he said. "It was unbelievable. I know it makes people smile. It's good that it takes the focus away from other problems out there."

### Quiet, Please

Anaheim coach Mike Babcock, hoarse from shouting during the Cup finals, said he's been mostly a silent type around friends and family for the past several days.

He sounded raspy and spoke softly before Monday's game.

"I'm saving it for tonight. I've got a sore throat," he said. "Actually, people that know me and had to hang out with me have liked it the last day and a half."

### By the Numbers

Teams winning Game 3 of the finals have gone on to win the Stanley Cup in 47 of 64 years since the best-of-seven format was introduced in 1939.

That would give the edge to the Mighty Ducks, who beat New Jersey 3-2 in overtime in the third game.

But teams that fell behind 2-0 in the series have come back to win the title only three times, most recently Montreal in 1971. Since Anaheim lost the first two games in New Jersey, that should give the edge to the Devils.

Statistics aside, of course, there are still games to be played.

# New Jersey Devils Go Back Home Tied

**AP STAFF WRITER**

ANAHEIM, Calif.—The Devils hoped to carry the Stanley Cup back to New Jersey after a two-game trip to Anaheim. Instead, they go home knowing they'll have to make one more trip to California.

Another loss in overtime to the Anaheim Mighty Ducks, this time 1-0 Monday night, evened the Stanley Cup finals 2-2. Game 5 of the best-of-seven series is Thursday in New Jersey. Anaheim will host the sixth game on Saturday.

And it looked like the Devils would have an easy time when they got to the West Coast after sweeping the opening two games at home by 3-0 scores.

"They feel pretty good about themselves, and on the other side, we just blew a 2-0 lead," Devils goaltender Martin Brodeur said. "So it's kind of hard to bring any kind of momentum into Game 5. But we'll regroup, and these next two days will be to our benefit because it will allow us to relax. We're really not used to that kind of travel."

The goal post helped Brodeur get the game into

| FINAL | 1st | 2nd | 3rd | OT | T |
|---|---|---|---|---|---|
| New Jersey | 0 | 0 | 0 | 0 | 0 |
| Anaheim | 0 | 0 | 0 | 1 | 1 |

overtime, but he had no chance on a rebound shot by Steve Thomas 39 seconds into the extra session. Now the pressure has shifted to the Devils, in the finals for the third time in four years. They are 10-1 at home in these playoffs, but only 4-6 on the road. The Ducks are 8-1 at the Pond.

"It's really important for us to have that confidence that we're going to be hard to beat in our building," Brodeur said. "They didn't play very well there the first two games, and I'm sure it's in their minds. So hopefully we'll get that first goal."

Brodeur, who surrendered one of the cheapest goals in Stanley Cup history in Game 3 when he dropped his stick trying to clear a dump-in by Sandis Ozolinsh, nearly made an even more egregious flub 4:27 into the third period.

Ruslan Salei, who gave Anaheim a 3-2 overtime victory in Game 3, shot the puck off the corner

boards from the blue line. The puck took a crazy bounce and caromed parallel to the goal line. Brodeur bent down and scooped the puck up with his glove. It then popped out, but Brodeur—facing the goal—pulled it back with his stick before it trickled across the line.

"I'm just trying to stay in my net as much as I can because it's such a bad rink for bad bounces on the ice off the boards and off the glass," said Brodeur, who made 25 saves.

"I figured the puck was going to go around the boards and it didn't, but I was in good position and waited for the puck to come to me. When I went to grab it, it just bounced on me and hit the top of my glove. But I was in control."

It was only the sixth time in finals history that a team won 1-0 in overtime. The last time was June 8, 2000, when the Devils lost Game 5 at home against Dallas.

"You've got to forget it. They're a hot team in overtime and they're confident," Burns said. "We knew that, and we tried to change that invincible thing for them."

The Devils, who lost 18 of 24 faceoffs in the second period, were frustrated by Anaheim goalie Jean-Sebastien Giguere midway through the period when Brian Gionta redirected Sergei Brylin's shot right into the goalie's pads. Brylin lost 11 of 15 faceoffs through the first two periods.

With seconds left in the period, Jay Pandolfo chipped the puck ahead from the neutral zone. John Madden got a step behind defenseman Niclas Havelid before Giguere dropped to his knees to stop the breakaway.

Brodeur was saved by the post twice in a 3:16 span of the second.

Rookie Stanislav Chistov banged a 40-foot wrist shot off the right post; then Adam Oates slid one off the base of the left.

Right wing Michael Rupp, who had five goals in 26 games for the Devils this season, was inserted into the lineup for Jim McKenzie and played on a fourth line with Jiri Bicek and Pascal Rheaume.

"Rupp gave us a couple of good shifts," Burns said. "He's a big, strong kid who hasn't played in a while. So we debated it at the team lunch and finally we decided we would make that change."

The Devils had a couple of decent chances against Giguere in the fourth straight scoreless first period. Jamie Langenbrunner followed up his own 40-foot shot from above the right circle during a power play about eight minutes in and was denied on the rebound.

New Jersey's best scoring chance came about three and a half minutes later when Scott Gomez carried the puck down the left side and feathered a pass to Patrik Elias cruising down the slot. Elias had Giguere at his mercy, but fired a shot over the net.

STANLEY CUP

# Bounces Go Devils' Way During 6-3 Victory

**ALAN ROBINSON, AP SPORTS WRITER**

EAST RUTHERFORD, N.J.—So much for defense, so much for shutouts. The New Jersey Devils used crazy bounces and lucky breaks to turn around a tight series and get within a victory of the Stanley Cup.

Brian Gionta scored a goal and set up Jay Pandolfo for the go-ahead score—neither of which went off the Devils' sticks—in a decisive second period, and New Jersey beat the Anaheim Mighty Ducks 6-3 in Game 5 of the Finals on Thursday night.

After four games of limited scoring chances, minimal open ice, little scoring and excellent goaltending, all of the above vanished in a shootout that was the antithesis of the series to date.

"It was unbelievable," Devils goalie Martin Brodeur said. "What a weird game. I'm really thankful for my offense—and you usually don't say that too often, because they don't score too many goals."

What stayed the same in an unconventional game was the Devils' dominance on home ice. They've outscored the Ducks 12-3 while winning all three

| FINAL | 1st | 2nd | 3rd | T |
|---|---|---|---|---|
| Anaheim | 2 | 1 | 0 | 3 |
| New Jersey | 2 | 2 | 2 | 6 |

games at Continental Airlines Arena, and they're 11-1 at home in the playoffs. That matches Edmonton's 1988 record for home wins in a playoff year.

"We knew the pressure was on us tonight, and I think now we've put a little bit on them," Devils coach Pat Burns said. "The team rallied around each other, pushing each other and giving [heck] to each other, which made my job easier. I could see that on the bench."

What the Devils can see clearly is their third Cup in nine seasons. That would match the Detroit Red Wings for the most titles since the Edmonton Oilers won four straight in the 1980s.

"But it's the toughest [win] to get," Pandolfo said. "So close and yet so far away."

That's what the Devils found out only two years ago. This is the third time in four seasons that they've led the Finals 3-2; they beat Dallas in six games in 2000 but dropped the final two to Colorado a year later.

The Devils can raise the Cup by winning Game 6 Saturday night in Anaheim, where the Ducks won two closely played games in overtime to even the series.

"There were a few bounces that didn't go our way in Anaheim, but we didn't let that bother us," said Jamie Langenbrunner, who scored twice in the third period. "We didn't let that get us down. Tonight, we got a few fortunate bounces."

The only players working overtime Thursday were the goalies, Brodeur (20 saves on 23 shots) and Jean-Sebastien Giguere (31 saves on 37 shots). Giguere hadn't allowed more than three goals in any playoff game this spring, including seven overtime games.

"This goalie's been unbelievable for them. Hopefully, we got to his confidence a little bit," Pandolfo said. "We just seem to play well at home. Now we've got some confidence offensively maybe we can take to Anaheim."

The up-and-down, free-flowing game looked nothing like the first four games, when there wasn't a single goal scored in the first period. This time it was 2-2 after one period before the Devils retook the lead—not by putting the puck in the net, but by letting the Ducks do it for them.

Gionta, who had been without a goal in the playoffs, threw the puck toward the net from along the right-wing boards, and it deflected off Ducks forward Mike Leclerc's stick and into the net before Giguere could react at 3:12.

"That's an honest mistake. Mike's a hard worker. It's just unfortunate that it went into our net," said Giguere, who gave up four goals on the Devils' first 18 shots.

AP/WWP

AP/WWP

Samuel Pahlsson tied it just over three minutes later, but Pandolfo gave the Devils the lead for good at 4-3 midway through the period on a goal that was initially waved off by referee Bill McCreary.

Gionta was trying to get the puck down low when it deflected off Pandolfo's skate and past Giguere. McCreary signaled no goal, indicating Gionta had kicked the puck in.

Replays showed there was no distinct kicking motion by Gionta—the criteria the NHL uses to determine if a player is intentionally trying to

deflect the puck—and director of officiating Andy Van Hellemond called it a goal after watching a replay.

Ducks coach Mike Babcock said the goal should have counted.

"I mean, the kid tried to stop it, it hit his foot and it went in. Good break for them," Babcock said.

Langenbrunner added his 10th and 11th goals of the playoffs, the only scoring in the third period. Gionta assisted on the second one, giving him a three-point night.

# Kariya Lifts Ducks Over Devils

**AP STAFF WRITER**

ANAHEIM, Calif.—Anaheim star Paul Kariya was on wobbly legs, staggered by a thunderous hit that threatened to end his Stanley Cup finals. Then he made a comeback that stunned even the New Jersey Devils.

Just like the rest of the Mighty Ducks.

Kariya, leveled by a hit from Scott Stevens that was so hard it appeared he might be seriously hurt, returned to score his first goal of the series, and Anaheim evened the Stanley Cup finals by beating New Jersey 5-2 in Game 6 Saturday night.

Kariya was invisible for much of the series, unable to escape the Devils' trapping defense. But he set up two of the Ducks' three first-period goals with the breakthrough game coach Mike Babcock said was necessary from him to force a Game 7.

"It definitely showed a lot of grit for him to come back from a hit like that," Devils goalie Martin Brodeur said. "There's not too many guys who can do that."

What's equally remarkable is that his unexpected return mimicked that of his own team. The Ducks

| FINAL | 1st | 2nd | 3rd | T |
|---|---|---|---|---|
| New Jersey | 0 | 1 | 1 | 2 |
| Anaheim | 3 | 1 | 1 | 5 |

were wobbly themselves after being dominated in the first two games of the series, in danger of being swept, yet have forced a Game 7 it seemed unlikely they would ever see.

"One game to win Stanley Cup? You can't ask much more than that," Steve Rucchin said.

Rucchin scored the Ducks' first two goals about four and a half minutes apart in a fast-paced, all-offense first period that imitated the Devils' 6-3 victory in Game 5, when each team scored twice.

It was a familiar story for the Devils, who looked flat and uninspired at the start for a team in position to win the Stanley Cup. This is the second time in three years the Devils couldn't close out the finals in Game 6; they lost 4-0 in Game 6 to Colorado in 2001, then lost Game 7, too.

"We had a great opportunity to finish a series and let it slip away," Devils defenseman Scott

AP/WWP

Niedermayer said. "We just didn't play our game again. We weren't playing as a team, and that's how we have to be play in order to be successful."

Added Devils coach Pat Burns: "I was surprised we did that."

In what is threatening to become the first finals since 1965 in which the home team wins every game, Game 7 will be Monday night in the New Jersey swamp. The Devils have outscored the Ducks 12-3 there in three wins all decided by three goals apiece. Anaheim outscored New Jersey 9-4 in the three games at the Pond.

The Ducks, playing with the desperation expected of a team possibly playing in its last game, led 3-1 in the second period when Stevens leveled Kariya with a violent hit only a moment after the Anaheim captain had passed the puck.

Kariya was in open ice and was vulnerable, but clearly never saw Stevens coming, much like the Flyers' Eric Lindros didn't when he suffered a concussion on a similar hit by Stevens in a 2000 playoff game. Lindros ended up missing an entire season.

Kariya lay motionless for about a minute, the crowd at the Pond barely making a sound, before being helped up and taken to the locker room on legs so unsteady he needed help.

"I wasn't out cold," said Kariya, who began wearing a stronger helmet and a mouthpiece several years ago to help prevent concussions. "I was right there."

NHL officials issued a statement saying the hit was legal and not subject to a penalty, but Kariya clearly didn't agree.

"I didn't like the hit, obviously," Kariya said. "That's Scott Stevens's game. He's done that throughout his career. ... There's a fine line there."

Stevens said, "You can't let your guard down. Hey, it's a physical game out there."

After passing a quick series of tests and being cleared to return, Kariya was back in the game in less than five minutes. Only a few minutes after that, he was on the scoreboard for the first time in a series, only a day after repeatedly fielding questions as to whether his lost scoring touch might doom the Ducks. He had only one assist in the first five games.

Kariya took Petr Sykora's pass and, seeing open ice for one of the first times in the finals, let go of a hard slap shot from above the left circle that streaked by Brodeur and inside the far post.

AP/WWP

Rucchin, who got the memorable series-clinching overtime goal in Game 4 that sealed Anaheim's first-round upset of the defending champion Red Wings, got the first two goals as the Ducks improved to 11-1 in games in which they score first.

Rucchin scored at 4:26, taking Kariya's pass in the high slot and wristing a shot that deflected off Stevens and past Brodeur, who allowed five goals for only the second time in the playoffs this spring.

Rucchin beat Brodeur again with a shot from the right circle at 13:42, after Rob Niedermayer fought off two Devils along the boards for the puck and managed to get it out to Mike Leclerc, who got it

to Rucchin. It was Rucchin's seventh of the playoffs.

Anaheim also scored on the power play for the first time in 11 chances in the series when Steve Thomas put Kariya's deflection past Brodeur at 15:59. The Ducks got a second power play goal, by Sykora, early in the third period.

Brodeur was lifted after stopping only 17 of 22 shots. By contrast, Ducks goalie Jean-Sebastien Giguere had a relatively stress-free night, making 26 saves. His best came on a two-on-one break when he stopped Scott Niedermayer in the first, with the Ducks ahead 1-0. The Devils also couldn't convert two odd-man rushes about a minute apart in the second period, after Jay Pandolfo scored to make it 3-1.

# Devils Beat Ducks 3-0 to Win Stanley Cup

**ALAN ROBINSON, AP SPORTS WRITER**

EAST RUTHERFORD, N.J.—The New Jersey Devils, riding the greatest home-ice advantage in NHL playoffs history and a goal from one of the unlikeliest Game 7 stars ever, ended the Anaheim Mighty Ducks' surreal season and won the Stanley Cup with a 3-0 victory Monday night.

Mike Rupp, who had never appeared in a playoff game until being called on in Game 4, scored the first goal and set up Jeff Friesen for the other two. Friesen scored five goals in the series, all at home.

The Devils swept all four games at home—all with the second period proving decisive—in the first finals since 1965 and only the third in which the home team won every game. The Ducks rallied from 2-0 and 3-2 deficits to force a Game 7 by winning all three games in Anaheim.

Never has the home-ice edge been more important to a Stanley Cup winner. The Devils were a record 12-1 at home, allowing only 13 goals. They outscored the Ducks 15-3 in the four games in New Jersey, with each one decided by three goals.

| FINAL | 1st | 2nd | 3rd | T |
|---|---|---|---|---|
| Anaheim | 0 | 0 | 0 | 0 |
| New Jersey | 0 | 2 | 1 | 3 |

"We feel really at ease playing in our own building. The only reason we won the Stanley Cup is because we were so dominant in our own building," said goalie Martin Brodeur, who turned aside 24 shots in his third shutout of the series, all at home.

And who says there wasn't a triple crown winner this year?

The Devils, despite lacking the huge payroll and plethora of stars that Detroit has, won their third Stanley Cup in nine seasons—matching the Red Wings for the most since the Edmonton Oilers won their fifth Cup in 1990.

"This makes up for that bad time against the Colorado Avalanche," said Devils captain Scott Stevens. The Devils would have had a fourth Cup if

they hadn't lost a 3-2 series lead and the Cup to Colorado in 2001.

Brodeur outdueled Jean-Sebastien Giguere, whose remarkable goaltending earned him the Conn Smythe Trophy as most valuable player in the playoffs. He was only the fifth player to win the Conn Smythe on the losing team and first since Philadelphia's Ron Hextall in 1987.

A tearful Giguere never smiled as he accepted the MVP trophy to the boos of the New Jersey fans and the applause of the Devils players.

The Ducks had won only one previous playoff series in their 10-year history, upsetting the defending champion Red Wings and top-seeded Dallas Stars in consecutive rounds.

In the end, though, the jig was up for Jiggy and a straight-out-of-Hollywood season for the Ducks, who were trying to match the World Series champion Anaheim Angels by winning a totally unexpected championship seven months apart.

By preventing seventh-seeded Anaheim from becoming the lowest-seeded Stanley Cup winner ever, Rupp—an unknown name even to most Devils fans until a few games ago—wrote his name alongside Game 7 stars such as Henri Richard, Ray Bourque and Mark Messier.

Rupp hadn't played since early May and was skating only with the non-active players after practice before being unexpectedly pressed into the lineup by coach Pat Burns in Game 5. He played well enough to start getting regular shifts, but neither Rupp nor Burns could have expected this.

After both goalies enjoyed strong first periods, Rupp scored the pivotal first goal that has proven so important, with the Devils going 11-0 when they score first.

Only 2:22 into the second period, Scott Niedermayer's shot from the blue line was deflected by Rupp between Giguere's pads as the goalie moved to his left. Sensing how important the goal was, Giguere angrily pushed the puck out of his net.

"The second period has been our downfall here," said a dejected Adam Oates of Anaheim.

Niedermayer assisted on both goals to win his third Cup with the Devils and deny his brother, Anaheim forward Rob Niedermayer, his first. Before the series, their mother, Carol, said she hoped the Ducks would win so both sons could own the Cup.

Slightly less than 10 minutes after Rupp scored his first playoff goal in only his fourth playoff game, he gathered Niedermayer's rebound and tipped it to Friesen, who scored his fourth goal of the series but first since Game 2.

Friesen had three goals as the Devils won each of the first two games 3-0 against the Ducks, who were coming off a record 10-day layoff following their conference finals sweep of Minnesota.

Stevens, who as the captain was the first to skate with the Cup, handed it to Niedermayer, no doubt aware how difficult it was for the brothers to compete against each other for the same cherished prize.

One goal might have been enough for Brodeur on this night. Two probably seemed like 20 goals to Brodeur, who has now won an Olympic gold medal and a Stanley Cup in consecutive years. Brodeur's big-game experience meant all the difference as he became one of five Devils to win three Cups with the team.

# Regular Season Statistics

| Player (Skaters) | Position | GP | G | A | PTS | +/- | PIM | ATOI | PPG | PPA | SHG | SHA | SOG | SPCT |
|---|---|---|---|---|---|---|---|---|---|---|---|---|---|---|
| 26 Elias, P. | C | 81 | 28 | 29 | 57 | 17 | 22 | 18:05 | 6 | 8 | 0 | 3 | 255 | 11.0 |
| 15 Langenbrunner, J. | RW | 78 | 22 | 33 | 55 | 17 | 65 | 17:47 | 5 | 5 | 1 | 0 | 197 | 11.2 |
| 23 Gomez, S. | C | 80 | 13 | 42 | 55 | 17 | 48 | 16:00 | 2 | 10 | 0 | 0 | 205 | 6.3 |
| 12 Friesen, J. | LW | 81 | 23 | 28 | 51 | 23 | 26 | 15:32 | 3 | 5 | 0 | 0 | 179 | 12.8 |
| 25 Nieuwendyk, J. | C | 80 | 17 | 28 | 45 | 10 | 56 | 16:45 | 3 | 4 | 0 | 0 | 201 | 8.5 |
| 11 Madden, J. | C | 80 | 19 | 22 | 41 | 13 | 26 | 18:18 | 2 | 2 | 2 | 2 | 207 | 9.2 |
| 28 Rafalski, B. | D | 79 | 3 | 37 | 40 | 18 | 14 | 23:08 | 2 | 14 | 0 | 0 | 178 | 1.7 |
| 27 Niedermayer, S. | D | 81 | 11 | 28 | 39 | 23 | 62 | 24:29 | 3 | 7 | 0 | 0 | 164 | 6.7 |
| 29 Marshall, G. | RW | 76 | 9 | 23 | 32 | -11 | 7 | 13:38 | 3 | 8 | 0 | 0 | 113 | 8.0 |
| 14 Gionta, B. | RW | 58 | 12 | 13 | 25 | 5 | 23 | 14:47 | 2 | 1 | 0 | 0 | 129 | 9.3 |
| 4 Stevens, S. | D | 81 | 4 | 16 | 20 | 18 | 41 | 23:04 | 0 | 1 | 0 | 2 | 113 | 3.5 |
| 24 Stevenson, T. | RW | 77 | 7 | 13 | 20 | 7 | 115 | 11:53 | 0 | 2 | 0 | 0 | 85 | 8.2 |
| 18 Brylin, S. | C | 52 | 11 | 8 | 19 | -2 | 16 | 16:10 | 3 | 1 | 1 | 1 | 86 | 12.8 |
| 21 Rheaume, P. | C | 77 | 8 | 10 | 18 | -5 | 8 | 12:09 | 0 | 1 | 3 | 1 | 93 | 8.6 |
| 20 Pandolfo, J. | LW | 68 | 6 | 11 | 17 | 12 | 23 | 16:07 | 0 | 0 | 1 | 0 | 92 | 6.5 |
| 10 Tverdovsky, O. | D | 50 | 5 | 8 | 13 | 2 | 22 | 16:47 | 2 | 2 | 0 | 0 | 76 | 6.6 |
| 5 White, C. | D | 72 | 5 | 8 | 13 | 19 | 98 | 19:40 | 0 | 1 | 0 | 0 | 81 | 6.2 |
| 2 Smehlik, R. | D | 55 | 2 | 11 | 13 | -5 | 0 | 19:11 | 0 | 1 | 0 | 0 | 49 | 4.1 |
| 19 McKenzie, J. | LW | 76 | 4 | 8 | 12 | 3 | 88 | 7:41 | 0 | 0 | 0 | 0 | 42 | 9.5 |
| 9 Bicek, J. | RW | 44 | 5 | 6 | 11 | 7 | 25 | 11:48 | 1 | 0 | 0 | 0 | 63 | 7.9 |
| 3 Daneyko, K. | D | 69 | 2 | 7 | 9 | 6 | 33 | 15:36 | 0 | 0 | 0 | 0 | 38 | 5.3 |
| 6 Albelin, T. | D | 37 | 1 | 6 | 7 | 10 | 6 | 15:13 | 0 | 1 | 1 | 0 | 30 | 3.3 |

| Player (Goaltenders) | GP | W | L | T | GAA | TOI | SV | SV% | SO | TGA | TSA | PIM |
|---|---|---|---|---|---|---|---|---|---|---|---|---|
| 30 Brodeur, M. | 73 | 41 | 23 | 9 | 2.02 | 4374 | 1559 | .914 | 9 | 147 | 1706 | 10 |
| 35 Schwab, C. | 11 | 5 | 3 | 1 | 1.47 | 614 | 208 | .933 | 1 | 15 | 223 | 0 |
| 31 Ahonen, A. | 0 | 0 | 0 | 0 | 0.00 | 0 | 0 | .000 | 0 | 0 | 0 | 0 |